Table of Contents

Introduction

What Is Readers' Theater?

One good way to gain an understanding of readers' theater is to first get a clear picture of what it is *not*. Readers' theater is not a fully-staged production with sets, costumes, and dramatic action performed by actors who memorize lines from a script. Instead, a readers' theater performance is a dramatic reading, just as its name suggests. Readers are usually seated, reading from a script that is held in their hands or placed on a music stand in front of them. There may be minimal use of costumes or props, such as hats, a scepter or crown, or a simple backdrop to provide a suggestion of the setting and characters that the readers hope to bring to life for the audience during their dramatic reading.

Readers' theater offers all the enrichment of traditional theater productions, but without the logistical challenges that come with designing and building sets and creating costumes. Students are spared the stress of having to memorize lines, and can instead focus on developing a strong dramatic reading of the script.

How to Integrate *Readers' Theater* into Your Classroom

The *Readers' Theater* scripts may be used in a variety of settings for a range of educational purposes. Consider the following:

Language Arts blocks are ideal for incorporating *Readers' Theater* scripts, with their emphasis on reading aloud with expression. Many of the follow-up activities that accompany each script address key skills from the reading/language arts curriculum.

Content-Area Instruction can come alive when you use a *Readers' Theater* script to help explore social studies, science, or math concepts. Check the Table of Contents for the grade-level content-area connections in each script.

Integrated Thematic Teaching can continue throughout the day when you use *Readers' Theater* scripts to help you maintain your thematic focus across all areas of the curriculum, from language arts instruction through content-area lessons.

School Assemblies and Holiday Programs provide the perfect opportunity to showcase student performances. Consider presenting a *Readers' Theater* performance for Black History Month, Women's History Month, for parent evenings, or any other occasion when your students are invited to perform.

Teaching the *Readers' Theater* Units

The 15 units in this volume each include the following:

- A **teacher page** to help you plan instruction:

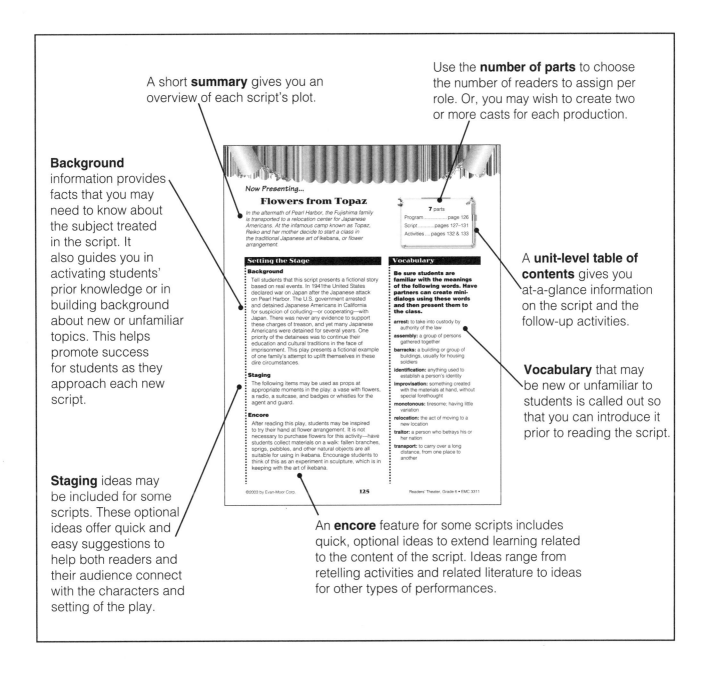

A short **summary** gives you an overview of each script's plot.

Use the **number of parts** to choose the number of readers to assign per role. Or, you may wish to create two or more casts for each production.

Background information provides facts that you may need to know about the subject treated in the script. It also guides you in activating students' prior knowledge or in building background about new or unfamiliar topics. This helps promote success for students as they approach each new script.

A **unit-level table of contents** gives you at-a-glance information on the script and the follow-up activities.

Vocabulary that may be new or unfamiliar to students is called out so that you can introduce it prior to reading the script.

Staging ideas may be included for some scripts. These optional ideas offer quick and easy suggestions to help both readers and their audience connect with the characters and setting of the play.

An **encore** feature for some scripts includes quick, optional ideas to extend learning related to the content of the script. Ideas range from retelling activities and related literature to ideas for other types of performances.

Within the teacher page image:

Now Presenting...

Flowers from Topaz

In the aftermath of Pearl Harbor, the Fujishima family is transported to a relocation center for Japanese Americans. At the infamous camp known as Topaz, Reiko and her mother decide to start a class in the traditional Japanese art of ikebana, or flower arrangement.

7 parts
Program .... page 126
Script .... pages 127–131
Activities .... pages 132 & 133

Setting the Stage

Background

Tell students that this script presents a fictional story based on real events. In 1941 the United States declared war on Japan after the Japanese attack on Pearl Harbor. The U.S. government arrested and detained Japanese Americans in California for suspicion of colluding—or cooperating—with Japan. There was never any evidence to support these charges of treason, and yet many Japanese Americans were detained for several years. One priority of the detainees was to continue their education and cultural traditions in the face of imprisonment. This play presents a fictional example of one family's attempt to uplift themselves in these dire circumstances.

Staging

The following items may be used as props at appropriate moments in the play: a vase with flowers, a radio, a suitcase, and badges or whistles for the agent and guard.

Encore

After reading this play, students may be inspired to try their hand at flower arrangement. It is not necessary to purchase flowers for this activity—have students collect materials on a walk: fallen branches, sprigs, pebbles, and other natural objects are all suitable for using in ikebana. Encourage students to think of this as an experiment in sculpture, which is in keeping with the art of ikebana.

Vocabulary

Be sure students are familiar with the meanings of the following words. Have partners can create mini-dialogs using these words and then present them to the class.

arrest: to take into custody by authority of the law

assembly: a group of persons gathered together

barracks: a building or group of buildings, usually for housing soldiers

identification: anything used to establish a person's identity

improvisation: something created with the materials at hand, without special forethought

monotonous: tiresome; having little variation

relocation: the act of moving to a new location

traitor: a person who betrays his or her nation

transport: to carry over a long distance, from one place to another

©2003 by Evan-Moor Corp. 125 Readers' Theater, Grade 6 • EMC 3311

- A reproducible **program** page provides an introduction to the script and a list of characters. Use this page to list the names of students who will read each role, and distribute it to your audience to enhance the theater-going experience.

- The **script** is the heart of the *Readers' Theater* volume. This is the reproducible four- or five-page text that students will read during rehearsals and performances. You may wish to read the script aloud to students before assigning parts and beginning rehearsal readings. Once you have read through the script as a group, you may wish to assign students to work independently in small groups while you interact with other student groups.

- Two or three pages of follow-up **activities** may be assigned once students have completed a first reading of the script. Activities are designed to be completed independently, and may be conducted while you provide individualized or small-group instruction or hold a rehearsal with another group of students.

Meeting Individual Needs

Struggling readers may be partnered with one or more stronger readers who all read the same role together. This group support is often enough to allow struggling readers to participate fully in the activity. Struggling readers may also be able to independently read parts that have a repeating refrain or a simple rhyme pattern.

Students acquiring English may benefit from using the same approaches as for struggling readers. In addition, you may wish to create an audio recording of the script to provide English learners the opportunity to listen to fluent English pronunciation of the script as they follow along with the written text.

Accelerated learners may be challenged to transform *Readers' Theater* scripts into fully-staged productions by adding stage directions, planning props and sets, and even developing or expanding the existing dialog. You might also use such students as "directors," helping to manage small-group rehearsals for class *Readers' Theater* productions.

Evaluating Student Performance

Use the templates provided on pages 5 and 6 to help students plan and evaluate their performances. You may copy and distribute the templates just as they are, or use them to guide you in leading a class discussion about the criteria for evaluating *Readers' Theater* performances. Students may also develop their own iconography (e.g., one or two thumbs up, thumbs down, 1 to 5 stars, etc.) to rate their own performances and those of their classmates. Encourage students to be thoughtful in providing feedback, stressing the importance of sharing ways to improve, as well as highlighting successful aspects of the performance. You may wish to conduct performance reviews during the rehearsal stage in order to give students an opportunity to incorporate suggestions for improvement. You may also wish to compare those comments to feedback following the final performance. Use the template on page 7 to conduct your own assessment of students' acquisition of language arts skills during *Readers' Theater* activities.

Pre-performance Checklist

Name _____

1. Did you listen to or participate in a first reading of the script?
   ☐ **Yes**
   ☐ **No** – Watch a group rehearsal if hearing the script aloud is helpful for you.

2. Did you highlight all your lines in the script?
   ☐ **Yes**
   ☐ **No** – Use a highlighting pen to go over all your lines.

3. Did you mark places where you must pause between lines?
   ☐ **Yes**
   ☐ **No** – Use a mark like this: / /

4. Have you collected any materials or props that you will use?
   ☐ **Yes**
   ☐ **No** – Ask your teacher or other cast members for ideas if you need help.

5. Have you chosen and practiced any movements, faces, or speaking styles you will use?
   ☐ **Yes**
   ☐ **No** – Ask your teacher or other cast members for ideas if you need help.

6. Have you practiced reading your lines with expression?
   ☐ **Yes**
   ☐ **No** – Try out your ideas with a partner or another cast member.

7. Have you participated in a rehearsal and gotten performance feedback?
   ☐ **Yes**
   ☐ **No** – Have a reviewer focus on your participation in the play. After you get feedback, find ways to make changes to improve your performance.

NOTE: Reproduce this page for students to use for peer evaluation of *Readers' Theater* rehearsals and performances.

Performance Review Template

Date: _____   Title of play: _____

☐ Rehearsal
☐ Performance

1. I am reviewing
   ☐ one reader   Name: _____ Role: _____
   ☐ the entire performance

2. I could see the reader(s).
   ☐ Yes
   ☐ Needs improvement   Name(s): _____

3. I could hear the reader(s).
   ☐ Yes
   ☐ Needs to speak more loudly   Name(s): _____

4. I could understand the reader(s).
   ☐ Yes
   ☐ Needs to speak more clearly   Name(s): _____

5. The reader(s) used good expression.
   ☐ Yes
   ☐ Needs to improve   Name(s): _____

6. The use of gestures was
   ☐ just right
   ☐ not enough; use more
   ☐ too much; use fewer   Name(s): _____

7. Some things that were done well:

   _____

   _____

8. Some things that could be done better, and some ideas for improving them:

   _____

   _____

NOTE: Reproduce this teacher page to assess student acquisition of the following *Readers' Theater* skills.

Assessing Oral Presentations

As you observe students during rehearsals or performances, focus on the following areas in assessing individual students.

Date: ______________________________

Title of play: ____

☐ Rehearsal

☐ Performance

Name: ________________________ Role: ________________________________

1. Student speaks clearly.	☐ Yes	☐ Needs improvement
2. Student speaks at appropriate pace.	☐ Yes	☐ Needs improvement
3. Student speaks fluently, using appropriate intonation, expression, and emphasis.	☐ Yes	☐ Needs improvement
4. Student enlivens reading with gestures and facial expressions.	☐ Yes	☐ Needs improvement
5. Student prepared and used appropriate props.	☐ Yes	☐ Not applicable
6. Student participated actively in rehearsals.	☐ Yes	☐ Needs improvement
7. Student contributed appropriately to this production.	☐ Yes	☐ Needs improvement

Other comments: ____

____

____

____

____

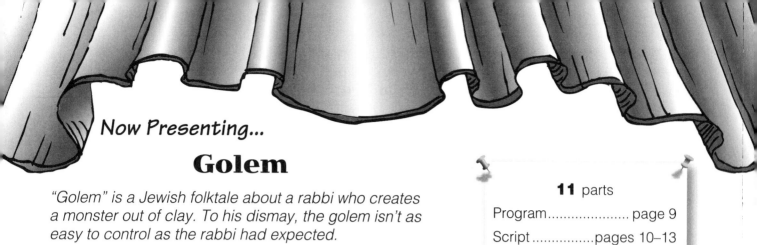

Now Presenting...

Golem

"Golem" is a Jewish folktale about a rabbi who creates a monster out of clay. To his dismay, the golem isn't as easy to control as the rabbi had expected.

Setting the Stage

Background

Lead students in a discussion about the nature of folktales. You might provide the following definition: "Folktales are popular stories that have no single author. They are told and retold by countless people. These stories are so popular that they influence modern forms of entertainment." As students read, ask them to think about characters from plays, films, novels, comic strips, or TV shows that remind them of the character Golem.

The word *golem* comes from a Hebrew word meaning "shapeless mass." This word later came to mean "a body without a soul."

Staging

The person reading the part of Rabbi Leib may use a cane or staff to show his age and authority. Have the person reading the part of Golem use a low, slow, almost mechanical voice to represent the inhuman creature.

Encore

After reading this script, students may enjoy reading David Wisniewski's beautifully illustrated version of this tale, *Golem,* which includes an extensive note with background information about the cultural context of the story.

Vocabulary

Introduce and discuss the following words before reading the script. Ask students to share what they know about what happens in the course of a trial, and then review the meaning of these words:

accuse: to blame; to bring formal charges of breaking a law

charge: to accuse of wrongdoing

defendant: a person who is accused in court of breaking a law

evidence: something presented in court to establish facts in a case

guilty: deserving blame or punishment; having one's guilt proven in court

justice: the administration of law to ensure fairness and the upholding of laws

plead: a statement made by a defendant in response to legal charges—usually "guilty" or "not guilty"

trial: a formal examination of facts by a court of law

Now Presenting...

Golem

In the city of Prague, Jews are unfairly and harshly treated. A rabbi creates a golem to protect the Jews. But who will protect them from the golem?

Characters

Narrator.................................... _____

Crowd...................................... _____

_____

_____

Emperor .... _____

Advisor to the Emperor .... _____

Rabbi Leib............................... _____

Jacob .... _____
(Rabbi Leib's assistant)

Golem .... _____

Isaac (a Jewish baker) .... _____

Guard .... _____

Golem

······················· Characters ·······················

Narrator	Jacob
Crowd	Golem
Emperor	Isaac
Advisor to the Emperor	Guard
Rabbi Leib	

Narrator: It is 1592. We are in Prague, a city in the land known today as the Czech Republic. For Christians, Prague is a center of learning and worship. There is a great deal of ignorance and prejudice, however. Jews are falsely accused of horrible crimes, and many fear for their lives. The Emperor is seeking advice on how to deal with the situation.

Crowd: The Jews must go! We demand justice!

Emperor: What is this terrible noise outside?

Advisor: The people are in an uproar. They believe that Jews are kidnapping their children. Worse, they accuse the Jews of drinking human blood!

Emperor: Is there any truth to these rumors?

Advisor: None that I know.

Emperor: Still, I have to do something. If I don't, the people will think I am weak. Let's punish Isaac the baker and make a show of it. Hopefully, the people will be satisfied with that.

Advisor: So be it. I will send the guards to get Isaac.

Narrator: At this time, there lived in Prague an old and respected rabbi, or spiritual leader. His name was Rabbi Leib, and he was very wise. Rabbi Leib knew things that had long been forgotten. He had the keys to life itself.

Rabbi Leib: Jacob! Wake up, quickly!

Jacob: *(sleepily)* Yes, Reb Leib. What's the matter?

Rabbi Leib: Come with me now to the river. I know it's late, but don't ask any questions. I'll explain everything to you on the way.

Jacob: Whatever you say, Reb Leib.

Narrator: Jacob and Rabbi Leib made their way to the river. There they formed the shape of a giant man out of clay. Rabbi Leib wrote the name of God on the giant's forehead, and it came to life. This was the mighty Golem. He was stronger than twenty men, but he barely had the intelligence of a child.

Rabbi Leib: Listen to me, Golem. You are here to protect the Jews, and you must follow my commands. Do you understand?

Golem: Yes, Master.

Rabbi Leib: Go into the city and hide. When the time is right, you will come to our rescue. Now go!

Golem: *(walking in a trance)* Golem follow commands . . . Golem hide and wait.

Narrator: The next day, Rabbi Leib attends the trial of Isaac the baker. Isaac is accused of mixing flour with the blood of Christians.

Emperor: Bring the defendant to me.

Isaac: Here I am, Your Majesty. What are the charges against me?

Emperor: Silence! I am asking the questions here, not you. How do you plead?

Isaac: Since I don't know the charges, how can I plead?

Emperor: Very well. There is plenty of evidence against you. Too much, in fact. There is no reason to go through it all. I find you guilty.

Guard: Your Majesty, we've just received dreadful news. A giant is rampaging through the city, and he's headed this way.

Emperor: A giant? Did I hear you correctly?

Guard: Yes, Your Majesty. It's . . .

Crowd: *(screaming)* . . . the GOLEM!!!

Narrator: At that moment, Golem comes crashing through the doors. He picks up two people, one in each fist, and is about to bash their heads together.

Crowd: Have mercy on us!

Golem: You cannot escape Golem! Golem will crush you!

Emperor: Guards! Bring this creature down immediately!

Guard: With what? Ropes and knives? You cannot mean it!

Emperor: Rabbi Leib, do something!

Rabbi Leib: Will you stop this mockery of a trial and leave the Jews in peace?

Emperor: Yes, anything you say. Just save us from this hideous monster.

Rabbi Leib: Golem, put those people down!

Golem: No!

Rabbi Leib: How dare you disobey me! I am your creator, and you must follow my orders. Let them down softly.

Golem: What will happen to Golem?

Rabbi Leib: Never mind, and do as I say!

Golem: Yes, Master.

Narrator: As Golem bends over and puts the two frightened spectators on the ground, the Rabbi quickly erases the name of God from his forehead with his staff. Golem falls to bits and pieces right on the spot.

Rabbi Leib: Let this be a lesson to us all. Those who harm others are no better than this mindless monster. May we all live in peace.

Name _____

Did You Get "Golem"?

How well did you understand the story? Check your comprehension by answering the following questions.

1. When and where does the folktale take place?

   _____

2. What is the problem at the beginning?

   _____

   _____

3. How does the Emperor respond to the problem?

   _____

   _____

4. What is special or unique about Rabbi Leib?

   _____

5. Why was Isaac's trial unfair? Give at least two reasons.

   _____

   _____

6. Do you think Rabbi Leib intended Golem to be so violent? Why or why not?

   _____

   _____

7. What do you think was going through Golem's mind at the end?

   _____

   _____

The Moral of the Story

Most folktales have a moral. The moral of the story is an important lesson. These lessons often give us warnings or advice.

What do you think is the moral of "Golem"? Choose from the following statements. Then tell why you think this is the moral. Give an example from the script. Finally, tell whether you agree with the moral and why.

Do unto others as you would have them do unto you.	**Revenge is not a solution to violence. It only leads to destruction.**
Self-control is more important than all the power in the world.	**We should choose our leaders carefully, because we are putting our lives in their hands.**

The Moral of the Story: _____

_____

_____

_____

Reason: _____

_____

_____

Personal Reaction: _____

_____

_____

Name _____

A Modern Version of "Golem"

If you were to update the story of "Golem," what changes would you make? Pretend that you are making a movie version. Show how the setting, characters, and plot might be changed.

Setting:

Prague, 1592 ⟶ _____

Characters:

Emperor ⟶ _____

Rabbi Leib ⟶ _____

Golem ⟶ _____

Plot:

I. Jews are falsely accused. ⟶ _____

_____

II. The Emperor holds a fake trial. ⟶ _____

_____

III. The Rabbi creates a monster out of clay. ⟶ _____

_____

IV. Golem barges into the trial and creates chaos. ⟶ _____

_____

V. The Emperor asks the Rabbi for help. ⟶ _____

_____

VI. The Rabbi takes the life-force from Golem. ⟶ _____

_____

Now Presenting...

Welcome to
Ellis Island

Tom and his older brother James have just arrived at the Ellis Island immigration center. They get separated, and Tom must go through his medical examination alone. Worse, he breaks out in a rash, and fears that he will be deported.

Setting the Stage

Background

Tell students that this play is set on Ellis Island, which was once an immigration center in the harbor of New York. The immigration center was opened in 1892. The first immigrant to walk through its doors was Annie Moore, a 15-year-old girl from Ireland. Many more immigrants followed, mostly from Europe. The flood of immigrants reached its peak in the early 1900s, but Ellis Island lost its importance as an entry point with the advent of air travel. It finally closed its doors in 1954, but reopened as a museum in 1968. Today it is one of New York City's most popular tourist attractions.

Staging

Consider using props to help identify the various characters, such as a legal pad and pen for the inspector, a stethoscope for the doctor, and a name tag for the volunteer.

Encore

If you and your students would like to learn more about the Ellis Island Immigration Museum, you may call the New York Park Service at (212) 363-3206 to request information about the museum's exhibits and educational programs.

Vocabulary

Introduce and discuss the following words before reading the script. Ask students to sort the words into two categories: words that might be found in a doctor's notebook, and words that might be found in the notebook of an immigration official. Then have students provide definitions for each of these words:

allergic: having an allergy—or extreme sensitivity—to a particular substance

citizen: one who is a member of a nation because of birth or naturalization

detain: to keep in custody

measles: an infectious disease characterized by small red spots on the skin

passport: a government document carried by travelers on international voyages

quarantine: a place where people with infectious diseases are kept in isolation

rash: a temporary eruption of bumps on the skin

Now Presenting...

Welcome to Ellis Island

Tom has just arrived in New York City from Ireland. Before he can leave the immigration center, he must pass a medical examination. Everything goes according to plan until the very last minute.

Characters

Narrator....................................... _____

Tom.. _____

James .... _____

Volunteer.................................... _____

Inspector .... _____

Doctor .... _____

Welcome to Ellis Island

·············· **Characters** ··············

Narrator	Volunteer
Tom	Inspector
James	Doctor

Narrator: In the spring of 1920, 13-year-old Tom O'Sullivan and his older brother James boarded an Irish steamship bound for New York City. After eight grueling days crammed into the hull of the ship, they catch sight of New York's harbor.

Tom: Look, James. Is it all these days at sea, or do I really see a giant lady in the middle of the bay?

James: Your eyesight is just fine, Tom. That there is what they call the Statue of Liberty. She's holding up a lamp to show the way. Look a little way farther. You see all those tall buildings just past her? Those are what they call "the mountains of New York." Some of them are even ten stories high!

Tom: They say that New York is the land of dreams. I heard that candy drops from the sky and falls right into your mouth!

James: You shouldn't believe everything you hear, Tom. In a matter of days we'll see what's true and what's not.

Tom: Why so long? We're here, aren't we?

James: First we have to go to Ellis Island. It's right over there by Lady Liberty. They'll check our papers and give us a look-over, from top to bottom.

Tom: What for?

James: They want to make sure we're fit and sound, I reckon. They can't let a whole ship of madmen loose in New York, now can they? Just be patient. As soon as our business is settled, we can board the train for Boston.

Tom: I can hardly wait. Ma must be worried sick about us.

James: Everything will be fine, Tom. Just do as you're told and answer all their questions the best you can.

Narrator: The steamship docked at Ellis Island, and the passengers made their way into the main building. They were all so excited that they forgot how tired and hungry they were. Volunteers were there to welcome them and explain what they were supposed to do.

Volunteer: This way, please. Please make a line and have your passports ready.

Tom: Can I go in with my brother?

Volunteer: I'm afraid not. You have to go in one by one.

Tom: What if we get separated?

Volunteer: You can wait for each other at the dock in New York, I suppose. Here, have a piece of chocolate while you wait. And welcome to America!

Tom: Is it all right if I eat this, James?

James: All right by me. Consider yourself lucky. I guess I'm too old for a treat!

Tom: *(smacking his lips)* I've never tasted anything like it. It's bitter and sweet at the same time. It's strange, but I think I like it.

Inspector: Next!

James: It's my turn, Tom. Remember what the volunteer said. If you get lost, I'll be waiting for you at the dock.

Narrator: Tom finished eating the chocolate bar, and waited his turn. As he waited, he started to get nervous and his face began to itch. It seemed like forever, but he was finally called into the Registry Room.

Inspector: Good morning, son. What's your name?

Tom: Tom O'Sullivan.

Inspector: Can you tell me why a young boy like you wants to be a citizen of the United States?

Tom: I've come to live with my mother and father. They live in Boston.

Inspector: And how do you plan to get there?

Tom: By train, with my brother. He's waiting for me downstairs.

Inspector: Why do you keep scratching your face, Tom? Is something the matter?

Tom: Just nervous, I guess.

Inspector: My goodness! Your face is covered with little red spots.

Tom: It must be from all the scratching.

Inspector: Try not to scratch it so much. That'll only make it worse. Let's have a doctor take a look, shall we? *(shouting into the next room)* Doctor, can you please come in here?

Doctor: *(entering)* Good morning, Inspector. What seems to be the problem?

Inspector: Young Tom here has a case of the itches. Would you mind taking a look?

Doctor: Oh, dear. It appears to be quite serious. How long have you had this condition?

Tom: It started as soon as I came in here.

Doctor: I rather doubt that. Maybe you've just noticed it, but I'll wager you caught something at sea. I pray for your sake it's not the measles. We'd better put you in quarantine, just to be safe. For the time being, you'll have to stay in the dormitory.

Tom: For how long?

Doctor: I don't know, son. Until we have a chance to give you some tests.

Narrator: The doctor used a piece of chalk to write the letter "F" on Tom's jacket, to stand for "facial rash." Tom had to spend the night in a crowded dormitory filled with other immigrants who were being detained for various reasons. In the morning, the volunteer he met the day before came to visit him.

Volunteer: Tom, what in the world are you doing here? I thought by now you'd be on your way to Boston.

Tom: That's what I was hoping too. The doctor made me stay because I have a rash.

Volunteer: Where?

Tom: On my face. Can't you see it?

Volunteer: No, I can't. Here, have a piece of chocolate while I go fetch the doctor. Once he sees the rash has gone, I'm sure he'll let you go.

Narrator: The volunteer went to find the doctor. While he waited, Tom nibbled on the chocolate bar. The volunteer was back with the doctor in less than half an hour.

Volunteer: As you can see, Doctor, young Tom is—Tom! What happened to your face?

Tom: It started itching again as soon as I ate the chocolate bar.

Doctor: I think I see what's bothering our little immigrant. Tom doesn't have the measles. He's just allergic to chocolate!

Tom: What does that mean?

Doctor: It simply means you're sensitive to chocolate. When you eat it, your body reacts by developing a rash. Mystery solved!

Tom: So can I leave now?

Doctor: As long as you promise not to eat any chocolate!

Narrator: Tom gathered his luggage and his papers, and then a ferry took him to the dock in New York City. To his relief, James was waiting for him, just as he had said.

Tom: James, I thought I'd never see you again!

James: I waited for you all night long. I couldn't leave without you, now could I? Here, I got a little treat for you. I know how much you like chocolate.

Tom: You can have it, James! I'll just have a piece of bread.

A Tour of Ellis Island

Each number on the map shows a place that immigrants had to stop on their way through Ellis Island. Write a short paragraph describing the process, based on the information shown on the map.

1 Entrance

2 Baggage Room

3 Stairway to the Great Hall

4 Medical Examination Room

5 Legal Inspection

6 Money Exchange

7 Exit

_____

_____

_____

_____

_____

_____

_____

_____

Name _____

Immigration to the United States
1820-1996

This table shows immigration statistics for the years 1820 through 1996. It presents the countries in alphabetical order.

Country of Last Residence	Number of Immigrants in U.S.
Austria	1,841,068
Canada	4,423,066
Germany	7,142,393
Hungary	1,673,579
Ireland	4,778,159
Italy	5,427,298
Mexico	5,542,625
Philippines	1,379,403
Soviet Union (former)	3,752,811
United Kingdom	5,225,701

Reorganize the countries in numeric order from highest to lowest. The first one has been done for you. When you are finished, total the figures and answer the questions.

Country of Last Residence	Number of Immigrants in U.S.
Germany	7,142,393
Total for All Countries	

1. How many immigrants came to the United States from Europe during this time period?

   _____

2. How many immigrants came from the Americas?

   _____

3. What is the average number of immigrants per year?

   _____

 Readers' Theater, Grade 6 • EMC 3311

Now Presenting...

Whiz Kid

Miguel is getting ready to appear on a TV quiz show with the help of his sister. He is overly confident, and doesn't bother to prepare for all the different categories of questions. Luckily, his sister is there to back him up.

Setting the Stage

Background

Ask students to tell about game shows they have seen on television. Talk about the different formats of these shows. Tell students that this play is about a boy who appears on a TV quiz show.

Staging

You may want to arrange the readers' chairs in front of the classroom to resemble the panel of a game show. Class members may take the part of the audience and clap after each contestant's answer.

Encore

After students complete the activity on page 34, you may wish to compile their questions and stage a class version of the "Whiz Quiz" game.

Vocabulary

Ask students to provide definitions for each of the following words without consulting a dictionary. The meanings of these terms are explained in the play. Have students check their definitions as they read.

collective noun: a word that names a group of items, such as a *flock* of geese

cranium: the skull

googol: the numeral 1 followed by 100 zeroes

hexagon: a geometric figure with six sides

polygon: a closed geometric figure with straight sides

quadrilateral: a geometric figure with four sides

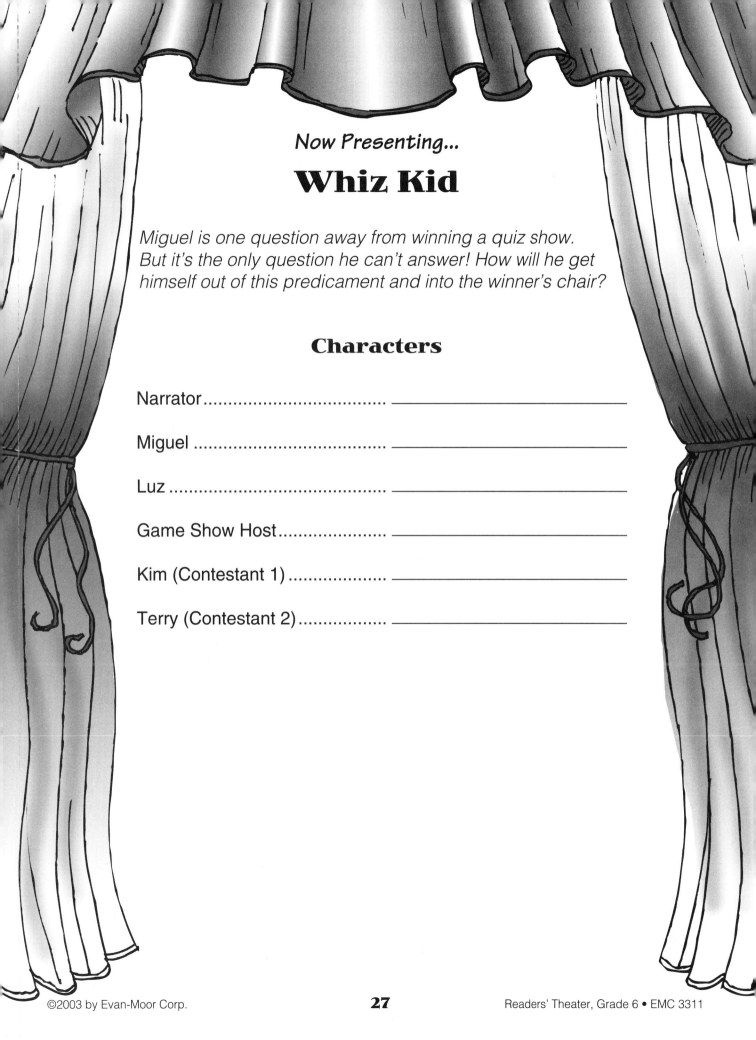

Now Presenting...

Whiz Kid

Miguel is one question away from winning a quiz show. But it's the only question he can't answer! How will he get himself out of this predicament and into the winner's chair?

Characters

Narrator .... _____

Miguel .... _____

Luz .... _____

Game Show Host .... _____

Kim (Contestant 1) .... _____

Terry (Contestant 2) .... _____

Whiz Kid

Narrator	Game Show Host
Miguel	Kim
Luz	Terry

Narrator: Today is a big day for Miguel. He's getting ready to appear on a TV game show called "Whiz Quiz." His sister, Luz, is helping him get ready.

Luz: C'mon, Miguel. The show starts in just three and a half hours.

Miguel: That's 210 minutes, or 12,600 seconds.

Luz: No matter how you measure it, we need to get ready.

Miguel: Go ahead, give me a few questions.

Luz: What's the tallest mountain in the world?

Miguel: Mt. Everest. Everybody knows that.

Luz: OK, that was just a warm-up. What do you call a group of bees?

Miguel: A swarm.

Luz: Ants?

Miguel: A colony.

Luz: Hawks?

Miguel: A flock?

Luz: Sorry! It's called a kettle of hawks.

Miguel: That's weird.

Luz: They're called collective nouns, or group terms. They're used for groups of animals. Sometimes they're used for other things too. We talk about a cord of wood, for example, or a ream of paper.

Miguel: They're not going to ask me questions like that. Give me some math questions. "Cool Math" is on every week.

Luz: Let's see. What's a polygon?

Miguel: A closed figure made up of line segments.

Luz: Good. Give me a few examples.

Miguel: Quadrilaterals are polygons with four sides. Squares and rectangles are two types. A hexagon is a polygon with six sides.

Luz: You're really good at math. You'll score high on that. But I think we should practice some of the other categories.

Miguel: OK, but we'd better practice on the way.

Luz: You're right. We only have 205 minutes left!

Narrator: At the TV studio, Miguel took his place on the stage. There were two other contestants, one on each side of him. As the lights dimmed, he scanned the audience to look for Luz. She waved to him from the back row just as the game got started.

Game Show Host: Good afternoon, and welcome to "Whiz Quiz," the show where kids are the experts. Today we have three contestants: Kim, Miguel, and Terry. I think you all know the rules of the game. You pick the category and I ask the questions. The player who answers the question correctly gets to answer the next question. You all get one chance to ask a member of the audience for help. Are you ready?

Miguel, Kim, Terry: Yes!

Game Show Host: Kim, you can get the game started. Pick a category from the board.

Kim: Let's do "The Human Machine."

Game Show Host: Very well. Here's the question: How many bones make up the human skull?

Kim: There are eight bones in the human skull.

Game Show Host: Sorry, Kim. That is incorrect. Miguel?

Miguel: Eight bones form the cranium that protects the brain, but there are a total of 29 bones in the skull.

Game Show Host: Right you are. You now have control of the board. Do you want to stay with the same category?

Miguel: No, let's switch to "Cool Math."

Game Show Host: OK, here we go. A "googol" is the number one followed by how many zeroes?

Miguel: There are 100 zeroes in a googol.

Game Show Host: Correct!

Narrator: Miguel answered all the questions in "Cool Math" correctly. Later, Terry took control of the board and correctly answered all the questions in "The Wonders of Nature." Kim was eliminated from the game, so Terry and Miguel were tied. To Miguel's surprise, the last category was "Collective Nouns."

Game Show Host: This is our last round. Terry, tell me what you call a group of lions.

Terry: A pride of lions.

Game Show Host: That's correct. Let's continue. What do you call a group of hawks?

Terry: Oh, I know this is a weird one. It sounds like something from the kitchen. Is it a skillet of hawks?

Game Show Host: I'm sorry, Terry. That was a good guess, but it's incorrect. Miguel, do you know?

Miguel: Yes, it's called a kettle of hawks.

Game Show Host: A kettle of hawks it is. And now for our tie-breaker. If you answer this question correctly, you'll be the winner of today's game. What do you call a group of whales?

Miguel: I know it can't be a school of whales. That'd be too easy. May I ask a member of the audience?

Game Show Host: Yes, you may.

Miguel: I'd like to ask my sister. She's sitting there in the back.

Game Show Host: Miss, would you like to try answering the question?

Luz: It's called a pod of whales. But "school" is correct too.

Miguel: I'll go with "pod."

Game Show Host: Miguel, your sister came to your rescue. You're the winner of today's game! How did you know your sister would be able to help you out?

Miguel: Intelligence runs in our family!

Name _____

Collective Nouns

Match the group term on the left with the noun on the right. Many of these terms appear in the play. Review the script for help if you need to.

1. batch of   ants

2. cast of   bees

3. colony of   cattle

4. cord of   paper

5. herd of   cookies

6. kettle of   hawks

7. pod of   lions

8. pride of   characters

9. ream of   whales

10. swarm of   wood

Trivia Test

This play included lots of trivia. Test your memory by answering these questions, taken from the script.

1. How many minutes are in three and a half hours?

   _____

2. What is the tallest mountain in the world?

   _____

3. What do you call group terms such as *swarm* and *ream*?

   _____

4. What is a polygon?

   _____

5. What do you call polygons with four sides?

   _____

6. What is a hexagon?

   _____

7. How many bones are in the human skull?

   _____

8. How many zeroes are in a googol?

   _____

Name _____

Quiz-Show Questions

Write questions and answers for an episode of "Whiz Quiz." Create two questions for each category. When you are finished, share your work with a partner. Quiz each other and keep score to see who wins.

The Human Machine

Q: _____

A: _____

Q: _____

A: _____

Cool Math

Q: _____

A: _____

Q: _____

A: _____

The Wonders of Nature

Q: _____

A: _____

Q: _____

A: _____

Collective Nouns

Q: _____

A: _____

Q: _____

A: _____

Now Presenting...

Romeo and Juliet

Shakespeare's play about two tragic lovers is perhaps the most famous love story in the world. It has been revisited and retold in numerous versions, and is especially popular with young audiences.

Setting the Stage

Background

With students, brainstorm a list of plays by William Shakespeare. Invite students to share what they know about the plot of *Romeo and Juliet*. Students may be familiar with this play through relatively recent versions, such as the classic 1961 musical *West Side Story* or the 1996 film version of *Romeo and Juliet* starring Leonardo DiCaprio and Claire Danes.

Staging

You may choose to provide masks, mock swords, and a goblet for students to use as props at appropriate moments.

Encore

Students may be interested in reading an unabridged play by William Shakespeare after reading this adaptation. You may refer them to *Stories from Shakespeare* by Marchette Chute or *Favorite Tales from Shakespeare* by Bernard Miles. These two books present selected plays by Shakespeare in the form of short stories. Reading these stories will help students familiarize themselves with a play's story line before attempting to read it.

Vocabulary

Teach or review the meanings of the following words. Then ask students how they think these words might be used in this play.

banish: to send away, often as a form of punishment

decree: an official order

desperate: in despair; without hope

destiny: fate; things that are predetermined to occur

embroil: to draw into a conflict or fight

endanger: to expose to danger or harm

fatal: resulting in death

fortune: luck or fate

grievance: a situation believed to be unfair and creating a reason to complain

kinsmen: relatives

slain: killed

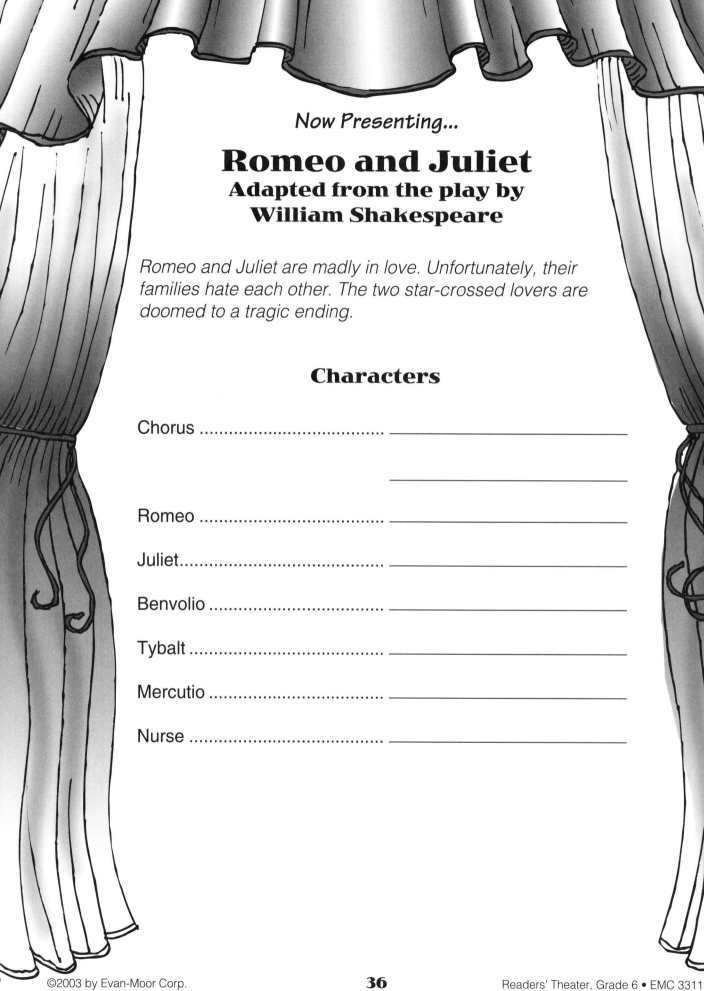

Now Presenting...

Romeo and Juliet
Adapted from the play by
William Shakespeare

Romeo and Juliet are madly in love. Unfortunately, their families hate each other. The two star-crossed lovers are doomed to a tragic ending.

Characters

Chorus .... _____

_____

Romeo .... _____

Juliet.. _____

Benvolio .... _____

Tybalt .... _____

Mercutio .... _____

Nurse .... _____

Romeo and Juliet
Adapted from the play by William Shakespeare

·························· **Characters** ··························
Chorus	Tybalt
Romeo	Mercutio
Juliet	Nurse
Benvolio	

Chorus: In the city of Verona, the Montagues and Capulets have been embroiled in a bloody feud. Four times they have fought in the streets, endangering innocent people. The prince is tired of the violence, and has decreed that anyone who fights in the streets will be punished by death. As our play opens, Romeo Montague dares to attend a costume party at the House of Capulet, home of his family's bitter enemies.

Benvolio: Look, Romeo, there is the fair Rosaline, whom you love so dearly. It's true she's pleasing to the eye, but she is only one flower in a garden of beauties. Come with me, and compare her with another that I know.

Romeo: One fairer than my love? Even the all-seeing sun has never seen Rosaline's match. Still, I'll go with you, only to prove you wrong.

Chorus: Romeo and Benvolio make their way to the dance hall, where Juliet and other guests have just entered. The music plays, and they dance.

Romeo: What lady's that who dances with Paris?

Benvolio: She's the very one I told you about. Her name is Juliet, and a Capulet; the daughter of your great enemy.

Romeo: It matters not. My heart has been struck, for I never saw true beauty 'til this night.

Benvolio: But you said that last week about Rosaline.

Romeo: Last week might as well have been another lifetime. Now please excuse me, my dear friend. I have a date with destiny.

Benvolio: I take leave against my better judgment. Fare thee well.

Romeo: *(to Juliet)* Please let me take your hand in mine, if I may be so bold.

Juliet: I see no harm in that. Even saints and pilgrims hold hands in prayer.

Romeo: Saints and pilgrims have lips too, do they not?

Juliet: Indeed they do, lips that they must use in prayer.

Romeo: Then be still, while my prayer takes effect.

Chorus: Romeo kisses Juliet. At that very moment, Juliet's nurse enters the scene, and the two must part. Later that night, Romeo appears beneath Juliet's window.

Romeo: *(out of Juliet's hearing)* What light through yonder window breaks? It is my lady! My love!

Juliet: *(to herself)* Ay, me!

Romeo: She speaks. I'll be quiet and listen to her words.

Juliet: O Romeo, Romeo, wherefore art thou, Romeo? If only you could change your name, or I mine. Then we could live together in happiness.

Romeo: *(louder, to Juliet)* I'll be whoever you want me to be.

Juliet: *(startled)* Romeo! What are you doing here? You will most certainly be killed if any of my kinsmen find you.

Romeo: I care not what happens. I'd rather die by the sword than starve for your love.

Juliet: Don't speak so lightly of love.

Romeo: I've never been more serious.

Juliet: Give me some sort of sign that your intentions are pure.

Romeo: Meet me tomorrow at the church. Friar Lawrence can marry us in secret. I know he will.

Juliet: You bring me so much joy, dear Romeo. Good night for now, good night! Parting is such sweet sorrow that I would say good night until the morning.

Chorus: The next day, while Benvolio and Mercutio are walking about the public square, they come upon Tybalt, a cousin of Juliet.

Tybalt: Where is the scoundrel named Romeo?

Benvolio: What business have you with him?

Tybalt: The business that I have is none of your business.

Mercutio: Tell us plain and simple what your grievance is, or else get out.

Tybalt: *(to Romeo, who has just entered the scene)* Ah, here he is. The one and only Romeo. Come here, lover boy. I have a special message for you. *(drawing his sword)*

Romeo: I have no quarrel with you. Therefore, farewell. I know you not.

Tybalt: That's no excuse for the injuries you have caused me and my family. Turn your face to me and draw your sword.

Mercutio: Tybalt, you ratcatcher! If you crave a fight, then fight with me.

Tybalt: Come and get me. *(They fight.)*

Romeo: Tybalt! Mercutio! The prince has banned all fighting in the streets. Stop! *(Tybalt stabs Mercutio.)*

Mercutio: *(looking at his wound)* I am hurt to the quick. Tybalt has made worms' meat of me. A plague on both your houses!

Romeo: My love for Juliet has made me too soft. Face me now, Tybalt. Either you or I or both must go. *(They fight. Tybalt falls.)*

Benvolio: Get away, Romeo! Tybalt is slain, and there are eyes all around. The Prince will sentence you to death if you are caught. Don't just stand there. Be gone!

Chorus: Later that afternoon, Juliet learns of the day's events through her nurse.

Nurse: Everything is undone. Tybalt is dead, and Romeo is banished.

Juliet: Did Romeo kill Tybalt?

Nurse: He did, alas. May he suffer for it.

Juliet: Hold your tongue! Tybalt would have killed Romeo if he could. My cousin is dead, but my true love is still alive. I weep, but not for Tybalt. My tears are for Romeo and my ill fortune.

Nurse: Listen, child. I have a plan. Drink this potion. It will put you into a deep sleep and slow your breathing to a near stop. Even the family doctor will think you have passed on. Tomorrow we'll all be attending your funeral. Your poor mother will be heartbroken, but I can tell you are set on escaping. I will send word to Romeo, and he will meet you in the tomb.

Juliet: Nurse, I am desperate. Give me the potion now that we may put your plan into motion.

Chorus: The next morning, Juliet's mother discovers her body and believes that she is dead. The house is filled with cries of grief, and Juliet is carried to her tomb. Romeo never receives the message from Juliet's nurse. He only hears what others believe—that Juliet is dead. He visits her tomb in the still of night, armed with a fatal dose of poison.

Romeo: O my love, you are as beautiful now as ever. It seems as if you have merely gone to sleep. I, too, will sleep, and we will embrace each other for eternity. Here's to my love! *(drinking the potion)* The drugs act quickly. Thus with a kiss I die. *(He falls.)*

Chorus: Juliet awakens a short while later, only to find the lifeless body of her true love beside her.

Juliet: Romeo, speak to me. Say some word. What's this? An empty cup? Did you drink poison and leave no drop for me? I will kiss your lips. Hopefully, some trace of poison will be left. No, I'll use your dagger instead. 'Tis better to take no chances. *(stabs herself and falls)*

Chorus: Juliet falls into Romeo's arms, and the tragic young lovers were never separated again. They were united in death as they never could be in life. The Montagues and Capulets finally ended their feud. They offered their truce to each other in memory of the star-crossed lovers.

Etched in Stone

Romeo and Juliet were buried together in the same tomb. What do you think might have been written on their tombstones? Write a fitting epitaph for each of the star-crossed lovers. *(An epitaph is an inscription on a tombstone in memory of the person buried there.)*

ROMEO   JULIET

In His Own Words

The script you just read is an adaptation of *Romeo and Juliet* by William Shakespeare. It was greatly shortened and the words have been simplified. Now read a few lines from *Romeo and Juliet* in their original form. In these lines, Romeo tells what he thinks about love.

Summarize Romeo's speech in your own words. In a few sentences, tell what you think Romeo is trying to express.

> Love is a smoke made with the fume of sighs:
>
> Being purged, a fire sparkling in lovers' eyes;
>
> Being vexed, a sea nourished with lovers' tears.
>
> What is it else? A madness, most discreet;
>
> A choking gall and a preserving sweet.

_____

_____

_____

_____

_____

_____

_____

_____

Now Presenting...

A Trip to Mars

A scientific expedition is sent to Mars in search of microbial life. The scientists find that life on Mars has been frozen in time, just waiting to be thawed.

Setting the Stage

Background

Ask students what they know about previous expeditions to Mars. You may need to prompt students by reminding them of the *Mariner* missions, the *Viking* missions, *Pathfinder, Sojourner,* and the *Mars Global Surveyor.* Students will find out more about these missions when they complete the activity on page 51.

Staging

You may want to provide students with model walkie-talkies to use for the scenes involving radio communications. You may also turn off the lights and have "light technicians" wave flashlights to simulate the scenes featuring space travel.

Vocabulary

Review or teach the meanings of the following words. Afterward, ask students to identify their part of speech. Have them identify the endings that indicate these words are adjectives.

automated: a system in which some or all of the processes are automatically performed or controlled by machinery or electronic devices

inflatable: something that can be inflated, or filled up with air

Martian: something that is from or lives on the planet Mars

microbial: relating to the microscopic organisms

navigational: relating to locating the position and plotting the course of an aircraft

organism: an individual plant, animal, bacterium, or other living structure with various systems that function together as a whole to maintain its life

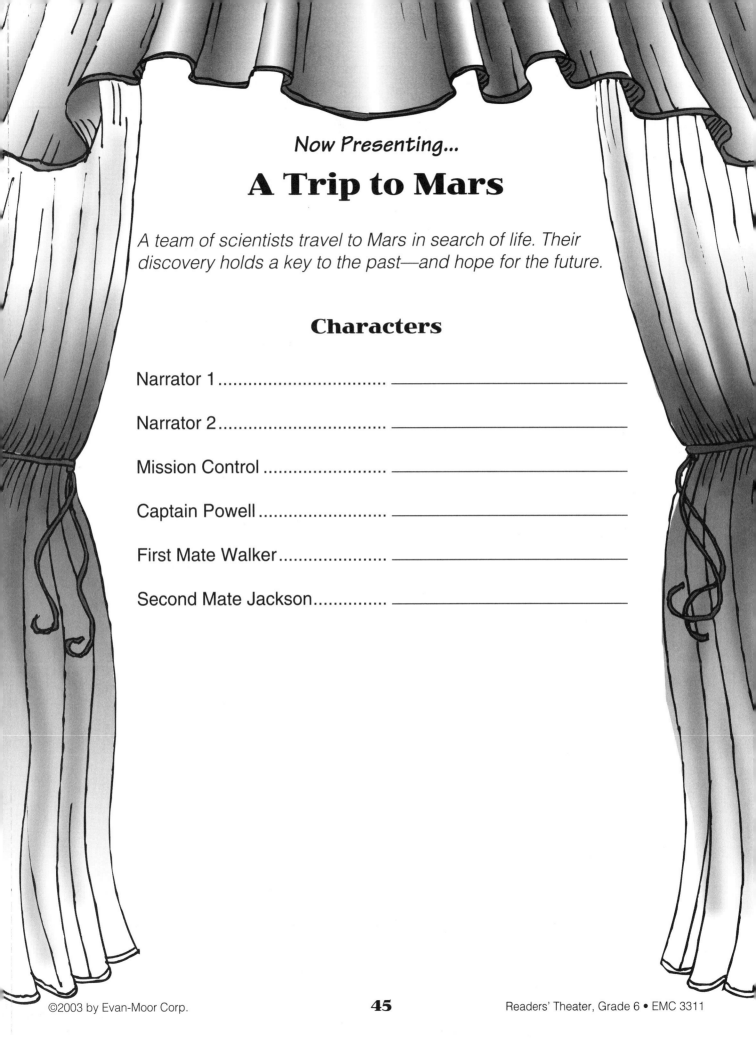

Now Presenting...

A Trip to Mars

A team of scientists travel to Mars in search of life. Their discovery holds a key to the past—and hope for the future.

Characters

Narrator 1 .... _____

Narrator 2 .... _____

Mission Control .... _____

Captain Powell .... _____

First Mate Walker .... _____

Second Mate Jackson .... _____

A Trip to Mars

························· **Characters** ·······················

Narrator 1	Captain Powell
Narrator 2	First Mate Walker
Mission Control	Second Mate Jackson

···

Narrator 1: The United States began sending space probes to Mars in 1965. Since then, we have learned that there was liquid water on Mars in the very distant past.

Narrator 2: But what about today? Could there be water under the Martian surface? If so, some form of life may be possible. As our play begins, a team of astronauts has just taken off from Cape Canaveral. Their mission: to search for life on Mars.

Mission Control: Congratulations, crew. You've just completed one full orbit around Earth. Take a good look—you won't be seeing that sight again for about three years.

Jackson: We have a wonderful view of southern Texas and the Gulf of Mexico. What a beautiful picture. I'm sure going to miss this place.

Mission Control: At your present speed, you'll be nearing the coast of South America in just a few minutes.

Walker: I think I already see it!

Mission Control: And they can probably see you. Wave out the window!

Walker: Hello, Brazil! And good-bye!

Captain Powell: Crew, prepare yourselves for another boost. As we pass Buenos Aires, we'll fire the rockets again and break away from Earth's gravity. Jackson, do the jets check out?

Jackson: Check!

Captain Powell: Walker, are you ready with the navigational system?

Walker: Ready, Captain!

Captain Powell: All right, crew. Countdown: 3 . . . 2 . . . 1 . . . Fire rockets!

Narrator 1: At that moment, the ship breaks away from Earth's gravity at a speed of 70,000 miles per hour. In about a week, it reaches the International Space Station, where it docks and refuels. After a final check, the ship takes off once again and follows a curving path toward Mars.

Narrator 2: Nearly six months and some 250 million miles later, the crew is orbiting the mysterious Red Planet.

Mission Control: Good morning, crew.

Captain Powell: Good morning, Mission Control. Shipmates Walker and Jackson are asleep in their pods. I didn't want to wake them because they've been working so hard.

Mission Control: What have you learned from the photos you've taken so far?

Captain Powell: Well, we've been photographing sand dunes with gigantic dark spots. These spots get bigger as the seasons change and the weather gets warmer.

Mission Control: What do you think it means?

Captain Powell: The expanding spots might be a sign that underground water is thawing. There's no way to know until we land and take some samples.

Mission Control: And that will be soon, with some technical know-how and a little bit of luck.

Captain Powell: I guess I'd better wake up the crew.

Mission Control: If they want to make any phone calls or send any e-mails, have them do it now. They'll be too busy once you start landing procedures.

Captain Powell: Copy. Over and out.

Narrator 1: The ship makes several orbits around Mars, getting closer each time. Landing pads are activated, and the ship softly touches the red sand.

Narrator 2: Before long, the crew contacts Mission Control to discuss plans for their first experiments.

Mission Control: As you know, the *Viking* missions tested Martian soil for signs of microbial life back in the 70s. But they barely scratched the surface. We need to go deeper this time. I think the sand dunes you spotted are a good place to start.

Captain Powell: Let's not waste any time. Walker, stay here and set up the inflatable laboratory. Jackson and I are going to take the rover out and collect samples. Do you think the laboratory will be ready to analyze the samples when we get back?

Walker: I hope so. Most of the lab is automated. The hardest part will be setting up the solar panels. I'll get started right away.

Captain Powell: Thanks, Walker. Are you ready Jackson?

Jackson: Yes, Captain. I've got all the drills and the sample boxes.

Captain Powell: Good! Let's go for a ride!

Narrator 1: Powell and Jackson drive across a windswept plain to the edge of a huge sand dune. Jackson inserts a probe into the crystalized sand. The probe reaches to a depth of several feet.

Jackson: Well, there's no water here. That was wishful thinking. It's just frozen sand and dirt. Mars looks like it's as dead as a doornail.

Captain Powell: Let's not jump to conclusions. Take two more samples and then we'll head back to the lab.

Narrator 2: Back at the laboratory, Walker puts the soil samples through several chemical tests.

Walker: There aren't any living organisms in this soil. If there were, certain kinds of gases would be present. Even simple cells breathe and digest food, but there's no trace of any such activity. So much for that. Now comes the fun part.

Jackson: Which is . . .?

Walker: We add water.

Jackson: It's like making pancakes!

Walker: More like planting seeds. Plant seeds don't appear to be alive. When you add soil and water, they come to life.

Jackson: You really think this will work?

Captain Powell: The experiment will speak for itself. Go ahead, Walker.

Narrator 1: Walker puts a small amount of Martian soil into a bowl and mixes it with liquid water from Earth. A short while later, the soil is analyzed by a computer.

Walker: Eureka! The computer detected carbon dioxide. That's a sign that some microbial organism down there is breathing. The computer also found several amino acids—the building blocks of life.

Jackson: Why couldn't we detect them before?

Walker: They were frozen in time. I can't wait to tell Mission Control!

Narrator 2: The crew radios Mission Control to tell them the good news.

Mission Control: This is amazing. Do you realize what this means?

Captain Powell: That life probably existed on Mars millions of years ago—maybe even further in the past. Some kind of climate change froze all the water, and life-forms have been preserved in the Martian ice.

Mission Control: Yes, all that is probably true. But that's not what I was thinking. I was thinking that this means there might be the possibility of bringing Mars back to life. This could be Earth's backyard garden, so to speak.

Captain Powell: I would say this trip has been a success.

Mission Control: A few grains of sand can turn out to be stepping stones for the whole human race.

Narrator 1: What will future expeditions to Mars reveal? Perhaps we will indeed reintroduce life to Mars.

Narrator 2: Maybe we will even live there ourselves some day. Only time will tell.

Name _____

Space Probes to Mars

Read the following chart. It gives information about space probes to Mars. Write a short paragraph about the exploration of Mars. Use some or all of the information from the chart.

Probe	Year	Mission
Mariner 4	1965	Took 22 closeup photos of Mars.
Mariner 6/Mariner 7	1969	Took more photos of Mars.
Mariner 9	1971	Took more than 7,000 photos of Mars.
Viking 1/Viking 2	1976	Landed on Mars. Analyzed rock samples and climate.
Pathfinder	1997	Landed on Mars. Analyzed rock samples and climate.
Mars Global Surveyor	1997	Photographed and mapped Mars' surface.

_____

_____

_____

_____

_____

_____

Name _____

Front-Page News

Write a summary of the discovery made by Captain Powell and his crew. Create a headline and write an introductory paragraph. Then draw a picture in the space provided and write a caption for it.

The DAILY News

Now Presenting...

Kids, Unite!

In this fictional story based on true events, Mary and her brothers join a strike to protest unfair labor conditions for child workers in the early 1900s.

Setting the Stage

Background

Ask students what they know about labor laws regarding children and teenagers. Make sure they know that there are laws limiting the number of hours that children can work, and that other laws prevent children below a certain age from working at all. It wasn't always so. At the turn of the nineteenth century, the abuse and exploitation of child laborers went unchecked throughout the United States. This was particularly a problem in mills and factories, where owners were unencumbered by labor laws and could dismiss labor leaders and strikers with impunity. The labor laws in place today are due to the efforts of those fearless Americans who risked life and limb to promote labor unions and new legislation. In this script, students will learn about some of these protections and the kid workers who fought for these rights almost a century ago.

Staging

You might want to help students create signs with slogans promoting the rights of child laborers. They can hold up these signs and wave them during the strike scene.

Encore

To learn more about workers' rights today, students can request information by writing to the U.S. Department of Labor, 200 Constitution Ave., NW, Washington, D.C. 20210, or by calling (202) 219-5000.

Vocabulary

Teach students the meanings of the following words. Then ask them to imagine how they might be used in a dialog between striking workers and the owner of a factory. Ask students to write snippets of such a dialog using some or all of the words.

association: an organization of people who share common interests

authorities: persons, especially those in government, with the power to enforce orders or laws

crippled: disabled

doffer: a textile worker who exchanges full bobbins or cones with empty ones

exploit: to make a profit from the labor of others without fairly compensating them

ingrate: an ungrateful person

justice: fair treatment

maim: to lose the use of part of the body through an injury; to cripple or disable

pneumonia: an infection of the lungs

replaceable: something whose place can be taken by another

subject: to cause to be under the control of

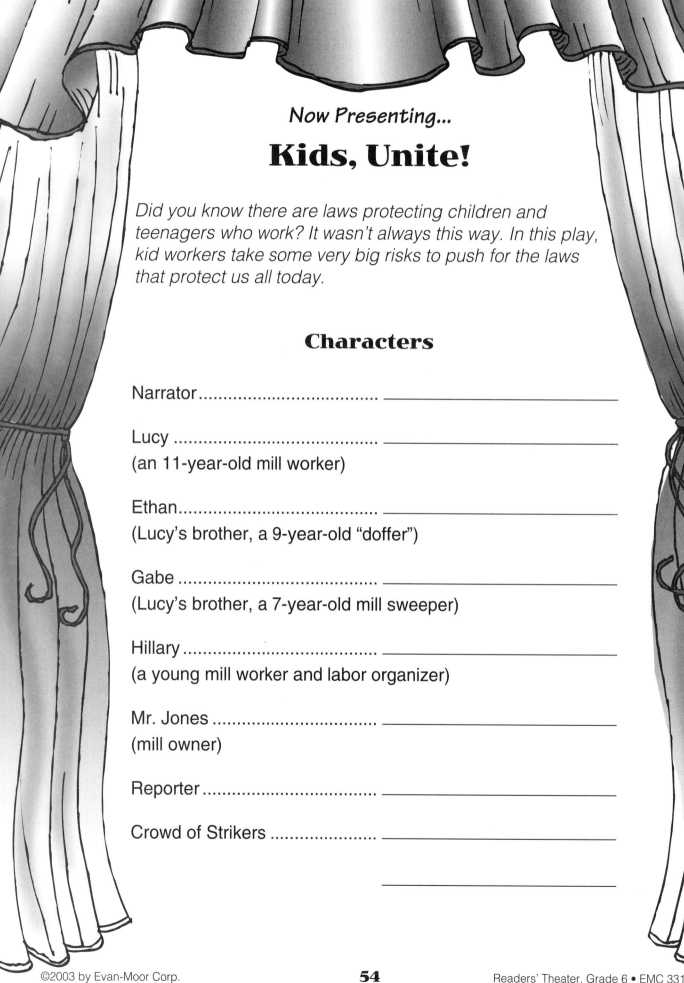

Now Presenting...

Kids, Unite!

Did you know there are laws protecting children and teenagers who work? It wasn't always this way. In this play, kid workers take some very big risks to push for the laws that protect us all today.

Characters

Narrator .... _____

Lucy .... _____
(an 11-year-old mill worker)

Ethan... _____
(Lucy's brother, a 9-year-old "doffer")

Gabe .... _____
(Lucy's brother, a 7-year-old mill sweeper)

Hillary .... _____
(a young mill worker and labor organizer)

Mr. Jones .... _____
(mill owner)

Reporter .... _____

Crowd of Strikers .... _____

_____

Kids, Unite!

···················· **Characters** ····················

Narrator	Hillary
Lucy	Mr. Jones
Ethan	Reporter
Gabe	Crowd of Strikers

Narrator: The year is 1903. Eleven-year-old Lucy Dobson and her two younger brothers are employed at a textile mill in a town near Philadelphia. In those days, it wasn't so unusual for young children to work in factories and mills. In fact, it was all too common. Children and teenagers had been subjected to back-breaking work under abysmal conditions since the beginning of our nation's history. By the early 1900s, many children were ready to fight back against their exploitation.

Lucy: Ethan, put another bobbin on top of the spinner. This one is full. But mind your feet when you climb on top of the machine.

Ethan: Yes, boss.

Lucy: Watch your language. Besides, if I don't look after you, who will? You're my own flesh and blood. And speaking of that, where's your little brother?

Ethan: He's asleep behind the mill. The poor little urchin is dead tired.

Lucy: Well, go find him and tell him to start sweeping. The floor is full of lint.

Ethan: And so is my hair and my mouth. I could use a good sweeping myself.

Lucy: Hurry up! If the boss-man finds him asleep he'll get fired.

Ethan: Lucy, I know it sounds awful—but that might be the best thing that could happen to Gabe. I think he's getting worse. I'm scared for him.

Lucy: Do you really think so?

Ethan: I'm afraid he'll get pneumonia, just like little James did. The air in this place is so stale and full of dust.

Lucy: Mr. Jones insists on keeping all the windows closed to protect his machines.

Ethan: And what about his poor workers? Did he forget we need to breathe?

Lucy: To him we're all replaceable.

Ethan: Well, we're not. I think we have basic rights as human beings, or at least we ought to.

Lucy: It sounds like you've been listening to Hillary! I heard that she is trying to start an association for the kid workers. I think maybe it's time for us to get involved.

Ethan: I think you're right.

Narrator: The next morning, Lucy and Ethan are up 5 a.m. They have to be at the mill by seven in the morning.

Lucy: Gabe, wake up. It's time to go.

Gabe: *(coughing)* Lucy, I can't. I'm too sick this time.

Ethan: Mr. Jones is going to fire us.

Lucy: Well, I'm at least going to put up a fight. I heard that the other kids are getting ready to strike.

Ethan: I say let's join them!

Gabe: Aren't we too young?

 Readers' Theater, Grade 6 • EMC 3311

Lucy: No, it's strictly a children's union.

Ethan: Then what are we waiting for? Let's meet Hillary on her way to work.

Lucy: Let's. Gabe, you stay here and rest. We'll see you tonight.

Narrator: Soon, Lucy and Ethan learned from Hillary about the strike that was set to begin the very next day. They joined with over 300 other children who refused to go to work, and the mill had to close. The children gathered in the city square, holding signs and eager to talk to anybody who would listen. A reporter from a local newspaper showed up to investigate the story.

Reporter: Why are you all on strike?

Hillary: It's our last resort. We've tried talking to Mr. Jones, the owner of the mill, but he won't listen.

Reporter: What are you asking for?

Lucy: The most important thing is that we want our hours reduced.

Ethan: For the same pay.

Hillary: Right now, we work about 65 hours a week. That's 13 hours a day. We don't have any time left over to wash and mend our own clothes.

Gabe: Or go to school.

Lucy: That's right. We want our hours cut so that we can at least go to school for one or two hours at night.

Hillary: And we also want safer conditions. Little ones get caught in the machines and wind up maimed or crippled.

Lucy: And one more thing. The overseers close all the windows. It's stifling hot, and the lint fills the air. We get sick from it all the time.

Reporter: Here comes the owner of the mill. Mr. Jones, what do you have to say about this strike?

Mr. Jones: I've never seen these kids in my life. None of them work for me. The ones who do work at the mill are all very grateful. At least they have a job.

Strikers: Less work! More school!

Mr. Jones: The kids at our mill get treated better than anywhere else. You ingrates!

Strikers: Less hours! More pay!

Mr. Jones: If we cut back on hours, the mill will lose money. This strike is costing us money.

Strikers: We demand justice!

Reporter: It looks like we have an uprising on our hands.

Mr. Jones: Exactly. I'm going to the authorities and having you all arrested!

Lucy: At least our complaints have been heard. We can't change the whole world overnight. As long as some progress is made, it helps us to have hope.

Narrator: The kid strike lasted for three days. In the end, Mr. Jones agreed to cut the workweek back to 55 hours, but he cut the kids' pay rate too. It took many other strikes for real change to occur. In 1916 one of the first labor laws was passed. It established fourteen as the minimum age to work in a factory, and it limited the workday to eight hours for children ages fourteen to sixteen. Since then, other laws have been passed to protect the safety and health of all workers. The kid strikes in the early 1900s show that workers of any age can make a difference if they unite and organize themselves.

Name _____

Wages Then and Now

Read the following statements. Then write a mathematical problem and its solution. Follow the example.

1. Lucy made one cent for every hour she worked. If she worked 13 hours a day, 5 days a week, how much did she earn

   a. per day?   **13 x $0.01 = $0.13**

   b. per week?   _____

   c. per month?   _____

2. Suppose Lucy made the current federal minimum wage, which is $5.15 per hour. If she worked 3 hours a day, 4 days a week, how much would she earn

   a. per day?   _____

   b. per week?   _____

   c. per month?   _____

3. Imagine that Lucy had a professional job and made $17.00 an hour. If she worked 7.5 hours a day, 5 days a week, how much would she earn

   a. per week?   _____

   b. per month?   _____

   c. per year?   _____

Name _____

Labor Terms

The terms in the word box are related to labor and unions. Complete the sentences with the following words. Use each word once.

boss	factory	grievance	management
negotiate	picket	strike	union

1. In a _____, people work on assembly lines with machines.

2. A _____ is a group of workers who organize themselves to improve their working conditions.

3. The _____ of a company includes its owners and supervisors.

4. A _____ is a complaint about wages or work conditions.

5. An informal word for a supervisor is _____.

6. A _____ is a refusal to work in order to get certain benefits from management.

7. Workers on strike form a _____ line to discourage the public from doing business with the company.

8. Workers and management can sometimes reach an agreement if they are able to _____.

 Readers' Theater, Grade 6 • EMC 3311

Name _____

Workers' Rights

What do you consider to be the most important rights that all workers should enjoy?
Create your own "Bill of Rights" in the spaces provided.

1. _____
   _____

2. _____
   _____

3. _____
   _____

4. _____
   _____

5. _____
   _____

6. _____
   _____

Now Presenting...

Balancing Act

Jerome and Lee are students at East Valley Middle School. Jerome thinks Lee is a "sissy," and Lee thinks Jerome is a "stupid jock." When they learn to look past the labels, they find out that they actually have something in common.

Setting the Stage

Background

Open a discussion about stereotypes by asking students what sort of images come to mind when they hear each of these labels: princess, sissy, nerd, jock, bully, and artsy type. Ask students to imagine what it feels like to be pigeonholed into one of these categories. Brainstorm reasons that people create stereotypes, and ways that we can all help to counteract them.

Staging

You may have characters walk on and off a "staging area" in front of the classroom as they are introduced by the narrator.

Vocabulary

Have students work with partners to look up the meaning of three of the following six words. Then have partners teach each other the meaning of the words they looked up.

admire: to have high regard for someone or something

apologize: to recognize and accept regret for a fault or a wrong

defensive: acting in a way to defend or justify your actions, often because of a feeling of being under attack

maturity: the state of being fully developed

right: something that belongs to a person by nature or by law

stereotype: a fixed idea about a person, group, or idea that allows for no individuality

Now Presenting...

Balancing Act

What's in a stereotype? The students at East Valley Middle School are about to find out.

Characters

Narrator.................................... _____

Jerome .... _____

Lee .... _____

Tony .... _____

Amber .... _____

Balancing Act

······················ Characters ·······················

Narrator	Tony
Jerome	Amber
Lee	

Narrator: Jerome and Tony are coming out of the locker room, suited up in their pads and helmets as they head to football practice. Jerome accidentally bumps into Lee, who is dressed in his gymnast's leotard as he heads for the balance beam in the gym.

Jerome: Excuse me, ma'am.

Lee: What's that supposed to mean?

Jerome: Oh, sorry! I thought you were a girl.

Lee: You should get your eyes checked.

Tony: Well, you're wearing nylons, aren't you?

Lee: They're called leggings. I'm on my way to the gym.

Jerome: You're on the gymnastics team?

Lee: As a matter of fact, I am.

Tony: Gymnastics. See what I mean? That's for girls!

Lee: You try jumping off a beam and landing on your feet. You'd be scared out of your wits.

Tony: I'm definitely not scared of you.

Lee: Yeah—well, you look pretty scary yourself with your padding and your face guard.

Jerome: Uh oh! Scaredy-cat's going to cry.

Tony: Get out your hankie.

Lee: Whatever.

Jerome: Yeah, c'mon, Tony. Let's get out of here. Ta-ta, Lee.

Lee: Arrivederci. That's Italian for "adiós."

Tony: Right. I'll see you in the funny papers.

Lee: Try the sports section—wearing the medal for the balance beam!

Narrator: Later that afternoon, Jerome is talking to Amber, the school president.

Jerome: Hey, Amber. Are you coming to the game on Friday night? I'm gonna take home the MVP trophy. I can just feel it.

Amber: Well, you definitely won't be getting any awards for maturity. I heard how you and Tony have been picking on Lee.

Jerome: What's the big deal, Amber? The guy's a sissy.

Amber: That is so uncool, Jerome. This is the twenty-first century. Your attitude is about five hundred years behind the times. I mean, does it really make you that uncomfortable that Lee does gymnastics? What are you afraid of?

Jerome: I'm not afraid of anybody or anything!

Amber: Yes, you are. Otherwise you wouldn't be so defensive. You're afraid of what other people think. Lee, on the other hand, doesn't seem to care a bit what you or anyone else thinks of him. He's going for what he wants, no matter what. He's independent. Those are qualities I really admire.

Narrator: Jerome couldn't stop thinking about Amber's comments. He certainly didn't want Amber to think he was uncool. But more importantly, he didn't want to be uncool. The next day, Jerome runs into Lee again outside the gym.

Jerome: Hi, Lee. How are you?

Lee: It speaks.

Jerome: You have every right to be ticked off at me. I've acted like a jerk.

Lee: Am I hearing correctly?

Jerome: Yes, you are. I can't apologize for Tony, but I apologize for myself.

Lee: Apology accepted. Being on the bad side of East Valley's star quarterback is not a good place to be.

Jerome: Well, don't thank me yet. I have a personal favor to ask.

Lee: What's that?

Jerome: Do you really speak Italian?

Lee: Well, I've heard enough at home to fake it pretty well.

Jerome: Yeah? Well, I'm going to Italy this summer. Do you think you could teach me a few things?

Lee: I could probably do that. Do you think you could show me the secret of your signature long-distance pass?

Jerome: I'll probably have to teach you how to hold the ball first, right?

Lee: Come on, dude—give me a break. I'm an athlete too, you know.

Narrator: Just then, Amber walks up.

Amber: Congratulations, Lee! You were awesome last night at the meet. Your routine on the balance beam was the best!

Lee: Hey, Amber—thanks a lot. It was cool that you could be there.

Amber: Are you kidding? I wouldn't have missed that for anything. You rocked!

Jerome: Sounds like you really are a star athlete, kid! Way to go!

Amber: Can I really believe what I'm hearing? Amazing, Jerome! It sounds like you actually do know how to listen to a girl after all. I guess maybe there really is hope for you.

Jerome: There is? So, will you come watch me play on Friday? Look how well it turned out for Lee when you went to watch him!

Amber: Sure, I'll come to the game. I don't know how much my support really had to do with Lee's great performance, but I'm definitely up for cheering on you and the home team. Do you want to come too, Lee?

Lee: To watch this jock get knocked around on a football field? It may not be graceful, but I guess it's athletic. Sure—I'll be there.

Jerome: Great! So where are you off to now, guys? There's still about twenty minutes of lunchtime left.

Amber: I was just going to check out the new routine that Lee's working on. I love to see how he pulls together all the different elements to make a smooth program.

Jerome: Hey, there's nothing like watching a great athlete at work. Can I come too?

Amber: Sure!

Lee: What are friends for, anyway?

Name _____

Stereotypes and Prejudice

This play is about stereotypes and prejudice. How would you define the following related terms? Use a dictionary if necessary, but write the definitions in your own words.

1. stereotype:

_____

_____

2. prejudice:

_____

_____

3. homophobia:

_____

_____

4. sexism:

_____

_____

5. racism:

_____

_____

6. diversity:

_____

_____

Name _____

What's Their Line?

Everybody has learned a lot in the course of this play except for Tony. He's still stuck in his old ways. In the speech bubbles, show how Lee, Jerome, and Amber might respond to some of Tony's inappropriate comments.

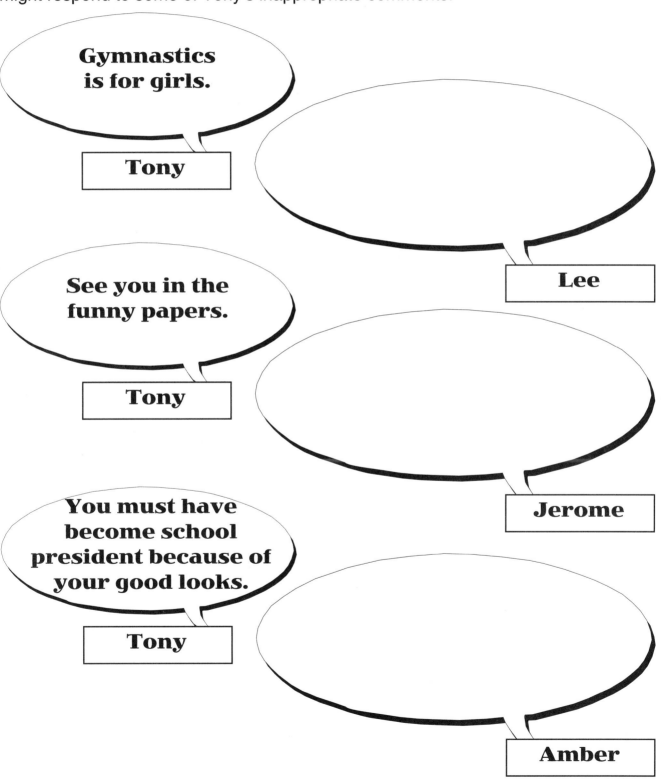

Gymnastics is for girls.

Tony

Lee

See you in the funny papers.

Tony

Jerome

You must have become school president because of your good looks.

Tony

Amber

Readers' Theater, Grade 6 • EMC 3311

Name _____

Down with Prejudice

Why is prejudice hurtful? Why are stereotypes limiting? Give five reasons why we should all fight prejudice and stereotyping.

1. _____

   _____

   _____

   _____

2. _____

   _____

   _____

   _____

3. _____

   _____

   _____

   _____

4. _____

   _____

   _____

   _____

5. _____

   _____

   _____

   _____

Now Presenting...

Sarah Winnemucca:
A Leader for Peace

Sarah Winnemucca was a Native American interpreter, writer, and diplomat. In this play, which is based on actual events, Sarah mediates a conflict between the U.S. Army and her fellow Paiutes. These negotiations established her credibility among whites and Indians as a mediator and diplomat.

Setting the Stage

Background

Give students background information on the reservation system in the United States. Explain: "As settlers moved west, they displaced Native Americans, who often fought back. Eventually, the U.S. government required that all Native Americans move to reservations, and the army was called upon to enforce this rule. Some Native Americans cooperated, but others did not. Sarah Winnemucca's father, for example, refused to live on a reservation. Young Sarah went to live with her grandfather, who believed the Paiutes should try to cooperate with whites. Later she lived with a white family in California and learned how to read and write English. As our play opens, Sarah has returned to her homeland in western Nevada with her brother Natchez."

Staging

Students may clap plastic bowls against the floor to mimic the sound of galloping horses at appropriate moments in the play.

Encore

Students might wish to learn more about Native American women who were effective leaders. Encourage them to check out *Sarah Winnemucca: Northern Paiute Writer and Diplomat* by Ellen Scordato and *Sacajawea* by Joseph Bruchac.

Vocabulary

Introduce and discuss the following words before reading the script. Then check comprehension by having students use each word in a sentence.

abide: to submit to

authorize: to give official approval or permission for something

criticize: to find fault with

interpreter: a person whose work is to translate spoken words from one language to another

intimidate: to use threats or violence in order to frighten someone

persuade: to use reasoning or urging to get someone to do something

prophetic: something that makes a prediction

provisions: food and other supplies

senseless: foolish; having no point or purpose

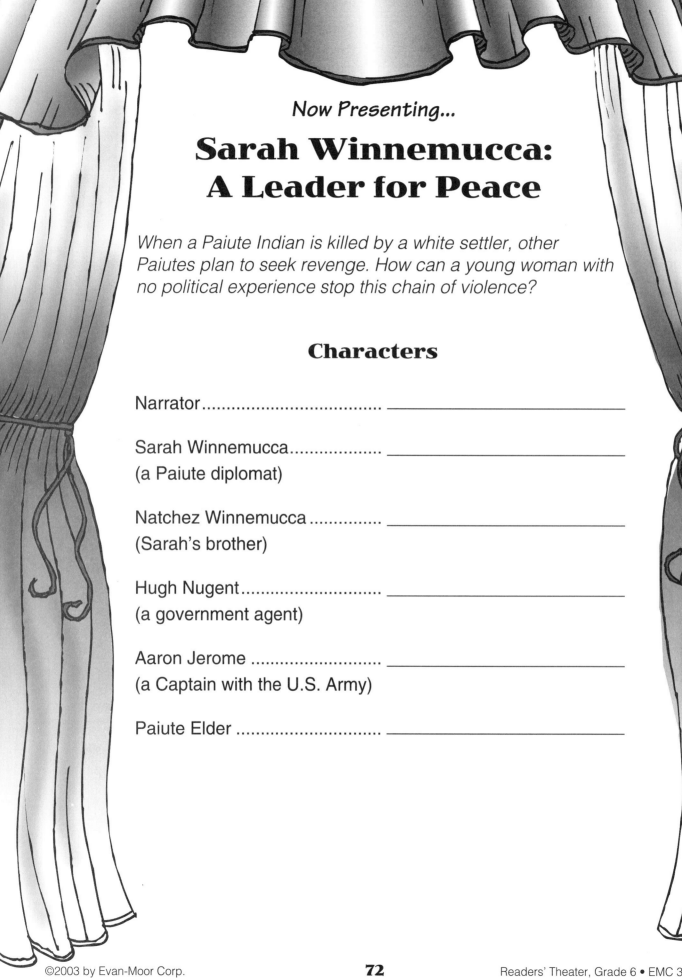

Now Presenting...

Sarah Winnemucca: A Leader for Peace

When a Paiute Indian is killed by a white settler, other Paiutes plan to seek revenge. How can a young woman with no political experience stop this chain of violence?

Characters

Narrator .... _____

Sarah Winnemucca .... _____
(a Paiute diplomat)

Natchez Winnemucca .... _____
(Sarah's brother)

Hugh Nugent .... _____
(a government agent)

Aaron Jerome .... _____
(a Captain with the U.S. Army)

Paiute Elder .... _____

Sarah Winnemucca:
A Leader for Peace

····················· **Characters** ·····················

Narrator   Hugh Nugent
Sarah Winnemucca   Aaron Jerome
Natchez Winnemucca   Paiute Elder

Narrator: It is 1866. Sarah Winnemucca and her brother Natchez live on a Paiute reservation in Nevada. They are discussing a horrible crime against another Paiute with one of their elders.

Paiute Elder: It is true, my children. Our dear brother has been killed.

Sarah: No! What happened?

Paiute Elder: Agent Nugent sold some gunpowder to our brother, even though it's against the law. Later, another white man killed our brother for carrying the forbidden gunpowder. The people are furious and want to take revenge against Nugent.

Natchez: If the people take revenge, we will surely be punished. The army will make our lives miserable. Sarah, what should we do?

Sarah: Let us go and warn Nugent. We will tell him to get away as quickly as possible.

Narrator: With that, Sarah and her brother jumped on their horses and rode like the wind to see Nugent. Natchez stood guard while Sarah tried to reason with the agent.

Agent Nugent: So, the Paiutes are coming to get me, are they? Let them! I'll show those red devils how to fight!

Sarah: Mr. Nugent, please try to see reason. This can only lead to disaster.

Agent Nugent: And whose fault would that be? I refuse to be intimidated by a band of unruly Indians!

Natchez: *(entering)* Sarah, I just heard that the Paiute warriors have raided a settlement and fatally wounded two white men. They should be here shortly.

Agent Nugent: You see? The Paiutes can't abide by the law. I'm going to Camp McDermit to see Captain Jerome. The army will teach you all a lesson you won't forget! *(leaves)*

Sarah: Oh, Natchez. What can we do? I've been having frightening dreams ever since the new moon. I pray they don't prove to be prophetic.

Natchez: All we can do is wait. We will know what to do when the time comes.

Narrator: The next day a messenger arrives at Sarah's camp. He brings with him an urgent message from Captain Jerome.

Paiute Elder: *(handing the note to Sarah)* Sarah, the note is addressed to you. Captain Jerome must know you are the only one here who can read and write English. Tell us what the note says.

Sarah: *(reading aloud)* "Miss Sarah Winnemucca—Your agent tells us very bad things about your people killing two of our men. I want to see you and your brother Natchez so we can talk. Yours, Captain Aaron Jerome."

Paiute Elder: You must write him a response without delay.

Sarah: What will I write with? We don't have any pens or ink.

Paiute Elder: Here, take this stick and dip it in fish blood. Use these to talk on paper. Tell Captain Jerome you will meet him tomorrow morning.

Narrator: After writing the note, Sarah and a small group of Paiutes rode their horses to Camp McDermit. Jerome and Nugent were waiting for them.

Agent Nugent: Here they are. Ask them to explain why the Paiutes senselessly killed two innocent men.

Captain Jerome: Quiet, Nugent. I've heard your side of the story. Now I want to hear theirs.

Sarah: Mr. Nugent probably left out a few details. Two days ago he sold gunpowder to a Paiute. The Paiute was killed by a white man for possessing gunpowder. That's why our warriors wanted to take revenge.

Captain Jerome: I see. Is there anything else you would like to add?

Sarah: Yes. Our people are nearly starving to death. Agent Nugent is supposed to supply us with provisions, but so far we have received nothing.

Captain Jerome: Your story is very convincing. The army is not authorized to get involved in Indian affairs, but perhaps I can help you. Would you be willing to return the favor?

Sarah: What do you want?

Captain Jerome: I hear that your father, Old Winnemucca, is in hiding. Do you know his whereabouts?

Sarah: I have not seen my father since my little brother was killed by soldiers years ago. After that, my father went to live in the mountains. He does not trust the white people, and wants to live as far away from them as possible.

Captain Jerome: I think your father can help to bring about peace in the settlement. The people respect him. Persuade your father to return, and we will provide you with cattle.

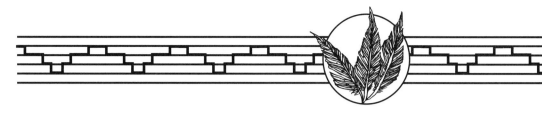

Agent Nugent: *(whispering in Jerome's ear)* Why give the cattle away for free, when we can sell them and make a profit?

Captain Jerome: Back off, Nugent! *(Nugent backs away, in silence.)* Well, Sarah? Do we have a deal?

Sarah: Captain Jerome, please excuse us while we talk in private. *(to the Paiutes gathered around her)* What do you think, my brothers and sisters?

Paiute Elder: I don't trust him. Why do they want to find your father? Maybe they're going to kill him! We've been lied to so many times before. Why believe them now? If you bring Old Winnemucca here and the soldiers kill him, his blood will be on your hands.

Natchez: Just because *some* white people are bad doesn't mean they are *all* bad. The army wants us to bring Old Winnemucca here to unite the people, just like Captain Jerome said. They want us to be peaceful. It's in their own best interest, because it's too much trouble to fight us all the time.

Paiute Elder: Perhaps you two are right. The life I once knew is fading fast. You young people can see the path to the future better than I. I will listen to your words. We will agree to the bluecoat's plan.

Natchez: Your words show that we still have much to learn from the wisdom you have gathered over the years. *(to Sarah)* Give Captain Jerome our answer.

Sarah: Captain Jerome, we accept your terms. My brother Natchez will leave tomorrow to go find Old Winnemucca. I'll stay here and inform the Paiutes of our decision. We will help each other, and in that way we will be partners.

Captain Jerome: You won't be sorry. You and your people will be cared for by the officers of the army.

Narrator: Natchez left the reservation to go find his father. Sarah stayed at Camp McDermit and worked as an interpreter. The army and the U.S. government did not keep all of its promises to the Paiutes, but Sarah continued to struggle on their behalf for the rest of her life. In speeches and in articles, she heavily criticized the reservation system. Today she is remembered as a fearless leader and a champion of human rights.

Name _____

Check Yourself

How well did you understand the play? Check your comprehension by answering the following questions.

1. When and where does the play take place?

   _____

   _____

2. How does the play open?

   _____

   _____

3. What would probably happen if the Paiutes took revenge on Agent Nugent?

   _____

   _____

4. What kind of person is Agent Nugent? How do you know?

   _____

   _____

5. What proposition does Captain Jerome make?

   _____

   _____

6. What skills and qualities make Sarah a good leader?

   _____

   _____

7. In your opinion, what are two possible criticisms against the reservation system?

   _____

   _____

Name _____

Sequence of Events

Number these events in the story in order. Review the script for help. The first one has been done for you.

_____ Natchez goes to look for his father.

___1___ Agent Nugent sells gunpowder to a Paiute man.

_____ Captain Jerome sends a letter to Sarah.

_____ Captain Jerome asks Sarah and Natchez to go find their father.

_____ Agent Nugent leaves the camp to save his life.

_____ Sarah and Natchez go to see Captain Jerome.

_____ Sarah becomes an interpreter at Camp McDermit.

_____ The Paiute man is killed for possessing gunpowder.

_____ Two Paiutes get revenge by killing two white settlers.

Now Presenting...

Arachne's Web

This play is based upon the Greek myth of Athena and Arachne. It explains why Athena became so enraged with Arachne that she turned her into a spider.

Setting the Stage

Background

Encourage students to share what they know about Greek mythology. You might have them summarize some of the stories they know or tell about the characters. Point out that the Greek gods lived in a heavenly palace called Mount Olympus. They were not "above and beyond" the affairs of mortals, however. To the contrary, they meddled in the lives of mortals quite frequently. In this play, the goddess Athena becomes jealous of a mortal named Arachne and decides to teach her a lesson.

Staging

You might provide two tapestries or cloth hangings to use as centerpieces for the play. Have the readers arrange themselves around the tapestries and gesture toward the hangings at the appropriate moments.

Encore

Students will surely be curious to learn more about Greek mythology after reading this play. Have them do research to find out more about other gods in the Greek pantheon, such as Zeus, Apollo, and Prometheus. Encourage students to compare and contrast the ways in which these gods have influenced human civilization.

Vocabulary

Introduce and discuss the following words before reading the script. Invite students to brainstorm synonyms and antonyms for each of the words.

arachnid: a member of the class of animals that includes spiders

arrogance: too much pride in oneself

artful: clever; crafty

conceit: too much pride in oneself

contradict: to say the opposite of what was said

descendant: a person born of a certain family or group

disrespect: rudeness; lack of respect

enrage: to make very angry

impertinence: rudeness

intimidate: to frighten

preoccupied: distracted by worry

worship: to show great honor and respect

Arachne's Web

The ancient Greeks wove countless tales about the gods on Mount Olympus. In this myth, the goddess Athena exacts revenge on a young weaver for her disrespect.

Characters

Narrator................................. _____

Athena.................................... _____

Arachne.................................. _____

Villager .... _____

Hera .... _____

Echo...................................... _____

Narcissus .... _____

Arachne's Web

······················· **Characters** ·······················

Narrator   Hera
Athena   Echo
Arachne   Narcissus
Villager

Narrator: Athena was the goddess of arts and crafts. The artisans of ancient Greece all worshiped her, and Athena gave them her blessings. There was one young weaver by the name of Arachne who did not pay the proper respect, however. This enraged Athena.

Athena: Arachne makes my blood boil with her impertinence. It's true that she is a very talented weaver, but she gives herself too much credit. Just listen to her boastful words!

Arachne: My tapestries are like works of art. It's truly amazing. I daresay that I am even better than Athena herself.

Narrator: Upon hearing these words, Athena flew into a rage. She swooped down from her throne on Mount Olympus and appeared before Arachne in all her terrifying glory.

Arachne: Heavens!

Athena: You wretched creature! How dare you compare yourself to me! It was I who invented the spinning wheel in the first place. You think you are so good? Then let us compete in a weaving contest. The villagers shall judge which one of us is best.

Arachne: I meant no disrespect, O mighty goddess, but can I help it if I'm the best? I'm only repeating what other people have said. I've even heard people say that I'm . . .

Athena: That's enough! I will see you tomorrow in the meadow. Be prepared to meet your fate.

Narrator: The next day, the villagers gathered in the meadow to see the weaving contest. They knew they were in for a treat, and they were not disappointed. Athena pulled threads from the clouds, and she used all the colors of nature. Her tapestry showed Hera, the queen of Mount Olympus, and Echo, another mortal who was disrespectful of the gods.

Villager: This is the most artful tapestry ever made. Hera and Echo seem to be walking, talking, living characters. Shhh! I think I can actually hear the voice of Hera. From the tone, it sounds like she is scolding Echo.

Hera: Echo, you try my patience with your endless chatter. I have never heard anyone in heaven or on Earth talk as much as you. You would do well to learn the art of silence.

Echo: Do you really think I talk that much? It all depends on your point of view. I only talk when there's something on my mind, and it just so happens that there is usually a lot on my mind. To me, silence is a sign of an empty mind, which is the same as stupidity. Words! Words! I love the sound of words—especially my own!

Hera: Now you've gone too far. You have contradicted me and questioned my authority. If you are so concerned with having the last word, so be it. From now on, you shall only be able to repeat what somebody else has said. Go ahead, say something.

Echo: Say something, say something.

Hera: And so shall it be, from now until the end of time.

Echo: Until the end of time . . . end of time . . . time.

Villager: I can barely believe my own senses! Pictures that walk and talk! What next?

Narrator: Arachne was not intimidated by this display. She licked her fingertips and set to work. Her fingers flew back and forth over the loom at lightning speed. Within a very short while, a picture began to emerge. It showed Echo spying on a beautiful young boy lost in the woods. The villagers were hypnotized by the scene.

Villager: This must be a continuation of Athena's story. I recognize Echo, but who is this boy? Echo is clearly in love with him, and who wouldn't be? He is beautiful to behold.

Narrator: To the villagers' amazement, Arachne's tapestry came to life. The boy in the scene was none other than Narcissus, a young man whose good looks were legendary. The figure in the tapestry began to speak. He was worried and preoccupied.

Narcissus: Where can I be? I've been lost in these woods for hours. Will anybody ever find me?

Echo: Find me!

Narcissus: Who else is here?

Echo: Here!

Narcissus: Oh, you took me by surprise. Why are you spying on me? Keep your distance. No, get away. Don't touch me!

Echo: Touch me!

Narrator: Narcissus fled, leaving Echo all alone. Then the scene changed as if in a dream, showing Hera on her throne. She was looking down at all this and took pity on Echo. She decided to punish Narcissus.

Hera: It is not good to waste such good looks. The finest women in the world throw themselves at Narcissus, but he always turns his back on them. Since he is so conceited, I will make him fall in love with himself. That will be an entirely fitting punishment.

Narrator: The last scene in the tapestry showed Narcissus gazing at his own image reflected in a river. He was so enchanted by himself that he stayed there forever, unable to break the spell.

Villager: Arachne has done it again. Not only is she the best weaver ever, but she is also the best storyteller. She took Athena's story and gave it a totally original ending. Arachne is hereby declared winner of the contest.

Athena: Aaaargh! You will pay the price for your arrogance and disrespect, Arachne!

Arachne: But I won fair and square. Your anger can't change that.

Athena: Perhaps not, but there are other things I can change—like your face!

Narrator: With that, Athena waved her hand over Arachne's face. It was immediately changed from the face of an attractive young woman to the face of an eight-eyed bug. Arachne shrieked in terror and ran for her life.

Athena: Not so fast, Arachne! Take this! And that!

Narrator: Athena cast a fine strand of silk and tripped Arachne as she ran. Arachne became entangled in a web. Her body shrank, stuck in the middle of the web. Now she had eight legs as well as eight eyes. Arachne had turned into a spider.

Athena: How do you like the end of this story, spider-woman? You will have all the time in the world to ponder its lessons!

Narrator: Arachne was and still is the best weaver of all time. Her art and her skills live on among the spiders of our world, her descendants. They continue to spin their webs today in her honor, which is why they are called *arachnids*.

Mythical Scenes

The tapestries made by Arachne and Athena amazed the villagers. Show what one of these tapestries might have looked like. Draw a scene from the story in the tapestry, and then label your drawing.

Name _____

Untangling "Arachne's Web"

How well did you understand "Arachne's Web"? Answer the following questions about the play.

1. Why is Athena so enraged at the beginning of the play?

   _____

   _____

2. Is Arachne the type of person who would be afraid to give a speech in front of a crowd of people? Explain your answer.

   _____

   _____

3. Which story does Athena tell in her tapestry? Which story does Arachne tell?

   _____

   _____

4. Many words in English have Greek roots. Based on this play, what would you guess the word *narcissistic* means?

   _____

   _____

5. What seems to be an important value in the culture of ancient Greece? Explain your answer.

   _____

   _____

6. Which character do you like the most in the story? Explain your answer.

   _____

   _____

7. This myth explains why spiders are such excellent weavers. In general, why do you think the Greeks created their myths?

   _____

   _____

Name _____

Character Traits

What words describe the characters in this play? Under each figure, write three words that describe that character. The first one has been done for you as an example.

Athena	Arachne
powerful	
authoritarian	
vengeful	

Echo	Narcissus

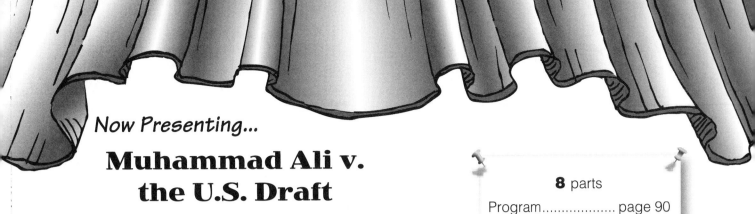

Now Presenting...

Muhammad Ali v. the U.S. Draft

Muhammad Ali was one of the greatest boxers of all time. In 1967 he took on his most formidable opponent—the U.S. government—when he refused to be inducted into the army.

Setting the Stage

Background

Encourage students to share what they know about the Vietnam War. You may use information from the time line on page 96 to help facilitate the discussion.

Staging

You may wish to use a bell or gong to introduce the fight scenes.

Encore

Students may be interested to learn more about the life of Muhammad Ali by viewing a video cassette of the feature-length film *Ali*. Actor Will Smith portrays the great fighter in this film, which includes events from this script, as well as other episodes in Ali's life.

Vocabulary

Ask students to provide a synonym or simple definition for each of the following words and use the words in a sample sentence. Provide assistance as necessary.

conscience: sense of right and wrong

exempt: to make free from a duty or obligation

hypocrite: person who is not sincere

induct: to take into the armed services

principle: rule of behavior or action

priority: to come first in order of importance

status: condition or position

verdict: decision of a jury

violate: to break a law or a rule or an agreement

Now Presenting...

Muhammad Ali v. the U.S. Draft

Muhammad Ali was one of the greatest boxers of all time. Today, he is remembered as a man of character who stood by his beliefs, no matter the consequences.

Characters

Narrator .... _____

Cassius Clay/Muhammad Ali .... _____

Sportscaster .... _____

Referee .... _____

Journalist .... _____

Draft Board Officer .... _____

Hawk .... _____

Dove .... _____

Readers' Theater, Grade 6 • EMC 3311

Muhammad Ali v. the U.S. Draft

····················· **Characters** ·····················

Narrator
Cassius Clay/Muhammad Ali
Sportscaster
Referee

Journalist
Draft Board Officer
Hawk
Dove

Narrator: In the early sixties, Cassius Clay was an up-and-coming young boxer. In fact, he hadn't lost a single fight as a professional heavyweight. On February 25, 1964, Clay was about to meet his biggest challenge to date. He was going up against Sonny Liston in Miami, Florida. At stake was the World Heavyweight Title. Liston was 31 years old. Clay was only 22.

Referee: In this corner, weighing in at 210 pounds, is Cassius Clay.

Clay: *(throwing jabs)* Float like a butterfly, sting like a bee!

Referee: And in this corner, weighing in at 218 pounds, is the World Heavyweight Champion Sonny Liston.

Sportscaster: Get ready to rumble!

Referee: Now shake hands and come out fighting.

Sportscaster: Clay is moving side to side like a dancer. Liston is moving in and—whoa! Clay throws a quick jab into Liston's face, and Liston throws a hard right that goes nowhere.

Narrator: Throughout the fight, Clay ducks Liston's punches by moving back quick as lightning at the last second. He takes a lot of hits too. His strategy is to tire Liston out, and it works. By the sixth round, Clay turns the tables on Liston and charges like a bull.

Sportscaster: Liston is looking tired. His face is puffy and bleeding. What's this? Liston has spit out his mouth protector! Ladies and gentlemen, Liston the champ has quit. Cassius Clay is the new world heavyweight champion! Let's hear what the champ has to say.

Clay: *(raising both fists over head)* I'm young, I'm handsome, I'm pretty, and can't possibly be beat. I'm the greatest!

Narrator: The day after the fight, champion Cassius Clay announced that he had become a Muslim and changed his name to Muhammad Ali. As a Muslim, Ali refused to be inducted into the U.S. Army. His refusal to fight in the Vietnam War in 1967 was front-page news across the country. "Hawks" supported our troops in Vietnam and jeered Ali. "Doves" were against the war and adopted Ali as a hero.

Journalist: We are here at a U.S. federal court in Houston, Texas. Heavyweight champ Muhammad Ali is on trial for violating the U.S. selective service laws by refusing to be inducted into the army. A crowd is on the steps of the courthouse, waiting for the verdict. Let's hear what they have to say.

Hawk: Ali is a disgrace to our country. We are fighting a war against communism, and we all have to do our part. If North Vietnam wins the war against South Vietnam, communism will spread throughout Asia. Eventually, it will spread to the U.S. If Ali isn't willing to fight in Vietnam, he isn't a true American.

Dove: That's baloney. America is the land of the free, isn't it? That means we're all free to follow our conscience and express our opinions. Ali is a true hero, because he's standing by his principles.

Journalist: A draft board officer is leaving the building. Sir, what can you tell us about the case of Muhammad Ali?

Draft Board Officer: Ali has been found guilty of violating the selective service laws. He has been sentenced to five years in prison and fined $10,000.

Journalist: What was his defense?

Draft Board Officer: He claimed that his status as a black Muslim minister made him exempt from the draft. The court finds no basis for this exemption.

Journalist: Here comes the champ himself. Mr. Ali, what's your reaction to the verdict?

Ali: I'm going to appeal the verdict because it's unjust. I cannot and will not fight in this war because I am 1,000 percent Muslim. The Koran—that's the Muslim holy book—forbids the taking of human life. Muslims are not allowed to participate in any war that is not in defense of the Muslim faith.

Hawk: Traitor! What about your fellow Americans?

Ali: I pledge allegiance to my black brothers. We were slaves 200 years ago. I'm not going to Vietnam to fight the white man's war.

Journalist: You realize you could go to jail for this.

Ali: I either have to obey Uncle Sam or I have to obey Allah, my lord. I choose Allah, because Allah controls the universe.

Journalist: What's your next step?

Ali: I post bail and then my lawyers are going to appeal the court's decision.

Narrator: Ali's case lingered in the court system for years. In the meantime, he was stripped of his heavyweight title and banned from boxing. Ali gave lectures at colleges and universities to spread his message. "Hawks" and "Doves" followed him wherever he went.

Ali: America needs to get out of Vietnam. We don't have any business there when we've got so many problems right here in our own country. We need to get our morals and priorities straightened out.

Dove: What should our priorities be?

Ali: Racism is a top priority for people of color. That's the real enemy facing the United States. Homelessness and poverty are two other enemies we face in this country. And drugs— we need to do everything we can to keep our kids away from drugs. We need to come together to solve these problems. Violence isn't a solution.

Hawk: But you make a fortune pounding people's faces into a bloody pulp. Why should we listen to you? You're a hypocrite!

Ali: You know I hate fighting. If I knew how to make a living some other way, I would.

Narrator: Finally, in 1970, a court order overturned Ali's suspension from boxing. Ali returned to the ring on October 26, 1970, in a famous fight with Jerry Quarry.

Sportscaster: Ali got off to a good start, but he's already slowing down. Quarry is pounding him. Wait a second . . . Ali is coming back with a flurry of punches. He connects, hitting Quarry over the eye.

Referee: Hold on Jerry, just sit still. That's one of the worst gashes I've ever seen. We have to get a doctor.

Narrator: Ali had brought his own team of doctors, but they were all black, and Quarry refused to be treated by a black doctor. The referee was forced to make a difficult call.

Referee: I've never seen a cut like this before. I can see right through to the bone. This fight is over. Ali wins on a technical knockout.

Narrator: Eight months later, Ali won the most important fight of his life. On June 28, 1971, the Supreme Court reversed his conviction for resisting the draft. Ali continued to perfect his boxing technique. From 1970 to 1981, Ali lost only five fights out of 32. He retired in 1981. A few years later, he was diagnosed with Parkinson's disease. What is Ali's legacy? He provided a positive image of a black man to his own community and to people around the world. Ali was a man of outstanding character who stood by his beliefs. Let's close our play with a few words by Ali himself on his personal philosophy.

Ali: Every living being was born to accomplish a certain purpose, and it is the knowing of the purpose that enables every soul to fulfill it . . . Everything I do has a purpose; all of God's beings have a purpose. Others may know pleasure, but pleasure is not happiness. It has no more importance than a shadow following a man.

Name ______________________________

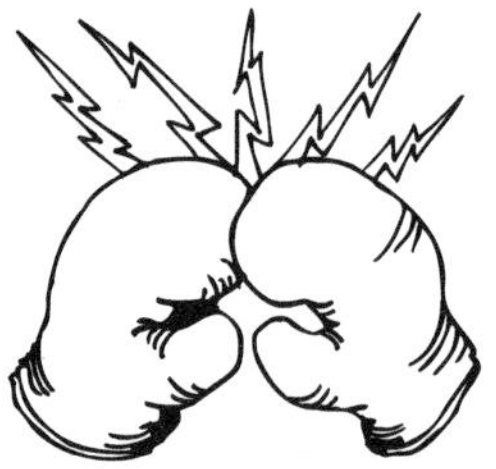

Chronology

This chronology shows important dates from Muhammad Ali's life. Fill in the blanks using information from the play. Write about all the important events that happened each year.

1964 — **Cassius Clay beats Sonny Liston.**

1967 —

1970 —

1971 —

1981 —

1984 —

War Slogans

What are other slogans each group might use? Write them below each group's poster.

HAWKS

DOVES

_____
_____
_____
_____
_____

Now Presenting...

To Tell the Truth

Jane can't resist telling tall tales about herself. Nicole and Amanda see through her lies and force her to get real.

Setting the Stage

Background

To open a discussion about the importance of honesty, ask students if they feel it's important that friends be truthful with each other. Encourage them to articulate how they feel about being treated dishonestly, and to think about whether they have ever been less than truthful in sharing information with friends. Ask students whether they think it's ever worth it to be less than honest in order to win friends or to get people to like you.

Staging

You might provide cell phones for students to use during the telephone conversations in the play.

Encore

Invite students to role-play other situations in which a character gets caught telling a tall tale. They might even develop such role-playing into skits to present to the class.

Vocabulary

To make sure that students are familiar with these words, ask them to give a synonym for each.

attractive: good-looking

celebrity: a famous person

genuine: true; authentic

glamorous: elegant; fancy

gorgeous: beautiful

illusion: a false impression

sincere: truthful; honest

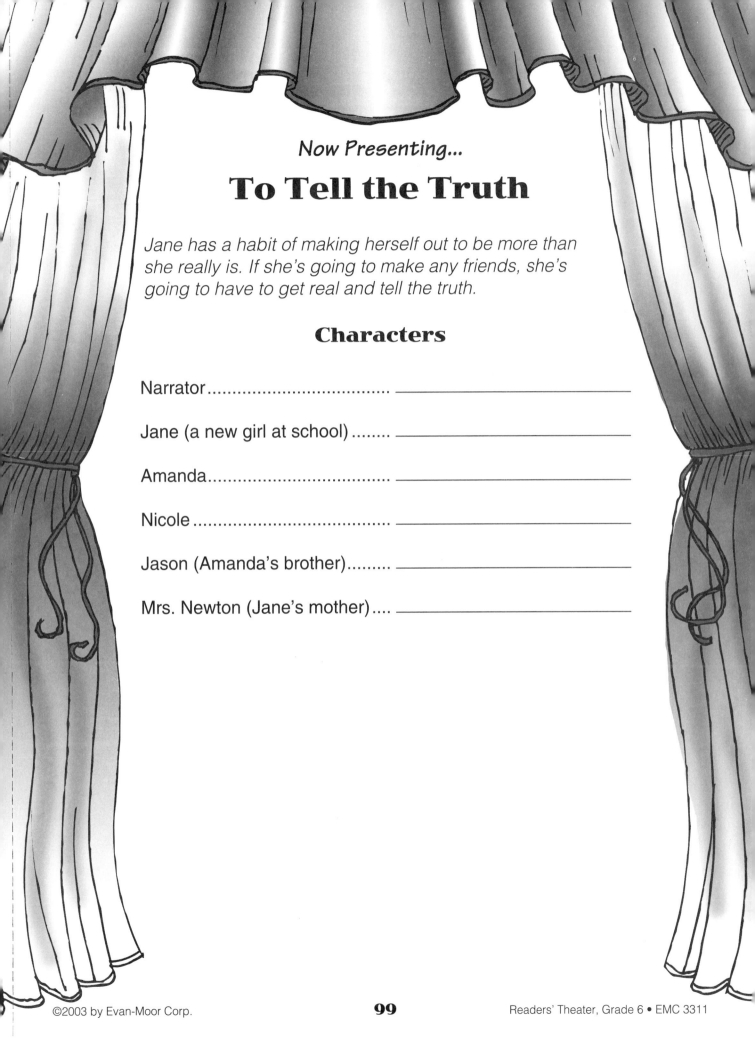

Now Presenting...

To Tell the Truth

Jane has a habit of making herself out to be more than she really is. If she's going to make any friends, she's going to have to get real and tell the truth.

Characters

Narrator .... _____

Jane (a new girl at school) .... _____

Amanda .... _____

Nicole .... _____

Jason (Amanda's brother) .... _____

Mrs. Newton (Jane's mother) .... _____

To Tell the Truth

············· **Characters** ·············

Narrator   Nicole
Jane   Jason
Amanda   Mrs. Newton

Narrator: Jane has just moved to Livermore, California. She's a new student at Junction Avenue Middle School. As our play opens, she's just met Amanda and Nicole during a break at school.

Jane: What a dreary school. This place is going to be hard to get used to.

Amanda: Where are you from?

Jane: Well, that's hard to say, because my job takes me so many places. New York, Los Angeles, Paris . . .

Nicole: The job? What *kind* of job?

Jane: Modeling and stuff like that.

Nicole: You work? How glamorous!

Jane: It's not, really. Oh, I suppose I meet some interesting people, but a lot of them are on star trips. I don't have time for their attitudes.

Amanda: I know what you mean. I hate people who are fake.

Jane: Of course, the work has its perks. I love all the free clothes and jewelry.

Nicole: Well, you probably won't find anything here that suits your tastes. Livermore is so simple. We always have to take the bus to the mall.

Jane: The bus? You must be kidding. You actually ride the bus with all those grungy people?

Nicole: Well, we really don't have any choice. Maybe we could all go together sometime.

Jane: Oh, maybe. I'm so busy, though, with my modeling and my boyfriend. He's in a band and . . . *(her cell phone rings)* Oh, that's probably him. Hello?

Mrs. Newton: Hi, Jane. How is school?

Jane: Oh, I've missed you so much. I've been thinking about you all day long.

Mrs. Newton: Jane, this is your mother.

Jane: I know, and I'm your baby girl. It's so nice to hear your voice.

Mrs. Newton: Jane, you're acting weird. I just called to see if you need a ride to work. I can drop you off on my way to the restaurant. Don't make me late for work!

Jane: Same time, same place?

Mrs. Newton: Yes, Jane. I'll pick you up in front of school.

Jane: *(click)* That was him. He's says the sweetest things, and he's so handsome! Well, I gotta go. See you tomorrow!

Nicole: Bye, Jane! *(to Amanda)* Wow, isn't this exciting? We have a celebrity in our very own school.

Amanda: I'm not so sure about that. It all seems too good to be true. I think maybe our new friend likes to tell stories.

Nicole: Oh come on, Amanda. Don't be jealous. It's not very attractive.

Amanda: Think about it. If she's a famous model, what is she doing in Livermore?

Nicole: I don't know. We can ask her next time.

Amanda: I just don't buy it. I don't want to be mean, but she's not exactly gorgeous. She's rather average-looking for a model. And isn't she way too young to have a boyfriend in a band?

Nicole: Who knows? Maybe she can get us into a show for free!

Amanda: We'll see . . .

Narrator: Later that afternoon, Jane is working at her job as a clerk at the local T-Mart. She is waiting on Jason, who is buying a pair of sneakers. Jane doesn't realize that Jason is about to catch her in the middle of a lie.

Jason: What's a cutie like you doing in a place like this?

Jane: Actually, my parents own the store. They own the whole chain, to tell the truth. I'm just helping out.

Jason: What are you doing after work?

Jane: I should tell you I have a boyfriend. He's the star quarterback on the football team.

Jason: Oh, well. No harm in asking, right?

Jane: Whatever.

Jason: *(on his cell phone)* Amanda, remember that new girl you told me about?

Amanda: You mean, the famous movie star?

Jason: Yeah. Well, I just saw her at T-Mart.

Amanda: What is she doing in a place like that?

Jason: Working. She says she owns the place, but I think she's really just a clerk.

Amanda: That girl couldn't tell the truth if her life depended on it. She's just a plain Jane, after all.

Jason: Yeah, well don't tell her that. It'll pop her bubble.

Amanda: Someone's got to pop it. Why not me?

Narrator: The next day, Jane runs into Amanda and Nicole in front of school. She is still under the illusion that her friends have fallen for all her lies.

Amanda: Hi, Jane. How was your date with your boyfriend?

Jane: Oh, it was wonderful. I hung out with him in the recording studio, and then he took me out for ice cream in his limo.

Amanda: Time to get real, Jane. My brother Jason saw you at T-Mart— selling sneakers!

Jane: There must be some kind of mistake!

Amanda: There's no mistake about it. You're a genuine fake!

Jane: I don't know what to say . . .

Amanda: That's the most sincere thing I've heard you say yet.

Nicole: Jane, it's OK if you're not rich and famous. Just try to be yourself.

Jane: I wouldn't know where to start.

Amanda: Just try saying something that's real.

Jane: I guess I'm just afraid. I'm afraid that people won't like me if they know who I really am.

Amanda: Well, at least you're being honest. That's a good place to start. Now, can we try this all over again from the beginning?

Jane: I'm willing to try.

Nicole: How about if we go out for ice cream today after school? And don't say you're busy!

Jane: To tell the truth, I don't have another shift at T-Mart until next week. I'd love to go out with you.

Amanda: For sure. That way you can get to know us and we can get to know who you really are. I have a feeling we're really going to like you after all.

Jane: I think having true friends like you will really be good for me. I think I'm going to like it here!

Readers' Theater, Grade 6 • EMC 3311

Name _____

True or False?

Read the following statements. They are all things that Jane would like other people to believe. What's the real story? Make the statements true by using phrases such as *really, actually, in fact,* and *in reality*. Follow the example.

1. Jane likes to think she is a famous celebrity.

   In reality, she's just an ordinary person.

2. Jane tells people that she has lived in New York and in Paris.

   _____

   _____

3. Jane pretends that she is a model.

   _____

   _____

4. Jane claims that she has a boyfriend in a rock-and-roll band.

   _____

   _____

5. Jane thinks she is drop-dead gorgeous.

   _____

   _____

6. Jane brags that her parents own the T-Mart.

   _____

   _____

7. Jane appears to be very self-confident.

   _____

   _____

8. Jane acts like she doesn't care what other people think.

   _____

   _____

Shades of Gray

PART I: Beauty is in the eye of the beholder. There are many shades of gray. Sort these words according to "degrees of beauty." Write the highest ranking word as 1, and the lowest ranking word as 7.

beautiful   gorgeous   hideous   plain   pretty   ugly   unattractive

1. _____   5. _____

2. _____   6. _____

3. _____   7. _____

4. _____

PART II: Now what about these words? They all have to do with degrees of truth. Write the words in order, from "beyond question" as 1 to "dishonest" as 7.

deceptive   false   probable   questionable   true   undeniable   unlikely

1. _____   5. _____

2. _____   6. _____

3. _____   7. _____

4. _____

Now Presenting...

The *Amistad* Case

In 1839 the United States was on the verge of a civil war. The passions of the time provided plenty of fuel for a legal battle involving 53 African refugees stranded in New England.

9 parts

Setting the Stage

Background

Tell students that this play is based on true events, although the facts have been condensed in this version. The play begins in 1839 on board the *Amistad,* a slave ship off the coast of New York. The Africans on board the *Amistad* contested their status as slaves, and argued their case all the way to the Supreme Court. At that time it was still legal to own slaves in the United States, although Americans were becoming sharply divided on the issue. Furthermore, it was illegal by then to take Africans from their homelands in Africa and sell them on the slave market. This turned out to be a critical factor in the *Amistad* case.

Staging

The judge may wish to pound a wooden mallet on a tabletop to announce the beginning of each court scene.

Encore

After reading the play, students may enjoy learning more about the *Amistad* case by reading *Amistad: A Long Road to Freedom* by Walter Dean Myers, *Rebels Against Slavery: American Slave Revolts* by Pat and Fredrick L. McKissack, and *Amistad Rising: The Story of Freedom* by Veronica Chambers. A feature-length film version of these historic events, directed by Steven Spielberg, is also available on video.

Vocabulary

Review concepts related to lower-court trials and the appellate system which eventually leads to the Supreme Court. Be sure students are familiar with the meanings of the following words:

attorney: a lawyer; a person trained in the law and authorized to act on behalf of another in a legal matter

crime: an act committed in violation of a law

penalty: a punishment set by the law

prosecution: the party—usually the State—that carries out criminal proceedings in court

sentence: the punishment for a crime as determined by a court

testimony: a sworn statement made in court

verdict: a decision or judgment by a judge or jury in court

witness: to furnish evidence or proof; give testimony; to provide oral or written evidence

Readers' Theater, Grade 6 • EMC 3311

Now Presenting...

The *Amistad* Case

When a ship full of Africans is discovered off the coast of New York in 1839, their fate is put into the hands of the American legal system.

Characters

Narrator .... _____

Judge .... _____

District Attorney .... _____

Pedro Montes (a slave trader) .. _____

Roger Baldwin (an attorney) ..... _____

Joseph Cinqué (an African) ...... _____

John Forsyth .... _____
(U.S. secretary of state)

Martin Van Buren .... _____
(U.S. president)

John Quincy Adams .... _____

The *Amistad* Case

····················· **Characters** ·····················

Narrator	Joseph Cinqué
Judge	John Forsyth
District Attorney	Martin Van Buren
Pedro Montes	John Quincy Adams
Roger Baldwin	

Narrator: In 1839 a U.S. Naval ship seized a suspicious-looking schooner off the coast of New York. It was a Spanish ship by the name of *Amistad*. On board were fifty-three Africans and two Spaniards. The Spaniards claimed that the Africans were slaves and had killed the entire crew. The full details of their story would not be revealed until the case was brought to court.

Judge: The court is here today to hear testimony in the case of United States versus *Amistad* Africans. The prosecution may now present its case.

District Attorney: Your honor, if it please the court, we would like to call our first witness, Mr. Pedro Montes. Mr. Montes, please raise your right hand. Do you swear to tell the truth, the whole truth, and nothing but the truth?

Montes: I do.

District Attorney: Do you recognize the defendants?

Montes: They are all slaves. I rightfully purchased them in Havana, Cuba. I had loaded them on the *Amistad* and was on my way to another town in Cuba, where I intended to sell them.

District Attorney: What happened to you and your crew during this trip?

Montes: The Africans came up from the hull of the ship in the middle of the night. Somehow they picked their locks and got loose. They found a crate full of machetes and used them to kill the crew.

District Attorney: Why didn't they kill you and your mate, José Ruiz?

Montes: They demanded that we sail east toward Africa. I tricked them by sailing north during the night. Fortunately, the U.S. Navy ship found us before it was too late.

Narrator: When it was time for the defense to present its case, attorney Roger Baldwin called Joseph Cinqué to the stand. Cinqué had been chosen by the Africans on board the *Amistad* as their leader. He spoke only Mende, an African language, so he had to speak to the court through an interpreter who could speak both Mende and English.

Baldwin: Cinqué, please tell the court where you are from.

Cinqué: I am a Mende from Mendeland, which you call Sierra Leone.

Baldwin: So you are not from Cuba?

Cinqué: No. I was only there for three days.

Baldwin: And you are not a slave?

Cinqué: No! I was a farmer in Mendeland. I had my own land, a wife, and children. The whites kidnapped me and the others you see here.

Baldwin: What happened to you and the other Mende?

Cinqué: You cannot imagine. The crew beat us, starved us, and worse.

Baldwin: Why did you attack the crew of the *Amistad*?

Cinqué: We were taken against our will. I would do anything to get back to my homeland, my family. Any man would do the same.

Baldwin: Would you like to make any other statements to the court?

Cinqué: We are men, like you. Give us back our freedom!

Baldwin: Your honor, the defense rests its case.

Judge: Both parties may now present their closing statements.

District Attorney: The prosecution has proven beyond the shadow of a doubt that these men are guilty of mutiny and murder. They should therefore be sentenced with the maximum penalty allowed by the law.

Baldwin: Your honor, as we have shown, the defendants are from Sierra Leone. There are no U.S. citizens involved in this case. How can they be tried in a U.S. court of law?

Judge: The court agrees with the defense. Mr. Montes is a Spanish citizen, and the defendants are from Sierra Leone. Furthermore, the crime happened at sea. This case does not in any way involve the United States or its interests. We order the defendants be returned to Sierra Leone, at the expense of the U.S. government, since they were taken from the *Amistad* by a U.S. Navy ship.

Narrator: The defendants jumped and cheered when they heard the verdict, but this was not to be the end of the *Amistad* case. Martin Van Buren, the president of the United States, was getting pressure from his advisors to bring the case to the Supreme Court.

Forsyth: Mr. President, the decision of the trial court in the *Amistad* case is most unpopular. Many people believe you should use your presidential powers to appeal the case to the Supreme Court.

Van Buren: The lower court has already ruled. Why should I concern myself with the fate of a few Africans?

Forsyth: The slavery question has brought this country to the verge of civil war. Southern slave owners are ready to separate from the Union. A more favorable decision in this case might help you when you seek reelection. Besides, the queen of Spain is unhappy with the decision as well. She wants the Africans returned to Spain.

Van Buren: Do you think the Supreme Court may reverse the decision?

Forsyth: There's a good chance. Five out of nine judges are slave owners.

Van Buren: Good point. Issue an immediate order that Cinqué and the others *not* be released from prison. The *Amistad* case will be tried one more time.

Narrator: Cinqué and his supporters were outraged when they heard the news. By this time, the *Amistad* case had received a lot of attention in the press. John Quincy Adams, a former U.S. president, offered his services as defense attorney. The date for the appeal was February 22, 1841. Members of the courtroom listened closely as the attorneys summarized their arguments.

Prosecutor: The defendants in this case are not human beings. They are slaves. Mr. Montes clearly established that he owned them at one time. As slaves, the defendants have no more rights than a beast of burden. They are the property of Spain, and should be returned to Spain. A Spanish court of law may then make a final decision in the case.

Adams: The Africans were brought into Cuba illegally. Therefore, Mr. Montes cannot claim that he ever rightfully owned them. The defendants were never slaves. They were born free, and have the right to their freedom. The men and women you see here are not criminals. Rather, they are more akin to the revolutionaries who fought against Britain during the American Revolution. They were fighting for their lives and their freedom. The United States is a land of justice, and justice demands that these men and women be set free.

Judge: The decision of the lower court is upheld. The defendants were taken from their homeland against their will. They had the right to fight back and resist. They are free to go. However, the U.S. government has no obligation to pay for their return trip to Sierra Leone.

Narrator: Cinqué and the other Mende were at last free. On the other hand, they had no money and were stranded in the United States. After all they had been through, they refused to give up. Cinqué learned English and told eager crowds his story. Eventually, he raised enough money from these lectures for a return trip. The *Amistad* captives finally returned to their homeland in 1842, three years after they had been kidnapped.

Name _____

Cause and Effect

Complete the table below to show how causes and effects are linked together in the play. The first one has been done for you.

Cause	Effect
Fifty-three Africans are kidnapped by slave traders.	**They kill the crew on board the *Amistad*.**
A U.S. Navy ship discovers the *Amistad* off the coast of New York.	
Attorney Baldwin presents overwhelming evidence in favor of the defendants.	
	The *Amistad* case is taken to the Supreme Court.
John Quincy Adams argues the case very effectively in court.	
	The Africans can at last afford the return trip to Sierra Leone.

Name _____

Arguments and Verdicts

What were the main arguments during the trial and appeal? What were the verdicts in each case? Complete the following table to summarize the main legal points.

	Trial Court	**Supreme Court**
Prosecutor's Argument		
Defense's Argument		
Verdict		

Now Presenting...

Akhbar the King

The king's behavior has been hard to explain lately. Things are not what they appear to be in this peaceful, but somewhat zany kingdom.

Setting the Stage

Background

Tell students that the play they are about to read is based on a folktale from India. Point out India on a world map. Explain that India is a modern democracy, but it was once ruled by kings. A king is a ruler with absolute power. That is, he can establish rules without the consensus of advisors or the general public. Many folktales and fairy tales feature kings and queens, often to point out their foibles and shortcomings. Introduce this play by telling students it's a lighthearted comedy about a king who had some very unusual ideas about how to run his kingdom.

Staging

You may wish to provide students with costume accessories such as crowns, canes, and robes to wear while reading their lines.

Encore

After reading the play, have students work in groups to write a script for another folktale they know. Then have groups read their scripts aloud for the class.

Vocabulary

Be sure students are familiar with the meanings of the following words, which they will revisit in the activity on page 124.

cautious: careful

commend: to praise; approve

indignant: outraged

peculiar: unusual

preposterous: ridiculous; outrageous

relieve: to reduce worry or pain

unpredictable: unable to foretell what will occur

Now Presenting...

Akhbar the King

Akhbar the King has been acting quite recklessly lately. Will he heed the advice of his wife and advisor before it's too late?

Characters

Narrator .... _____

Akhbar .... _____

Begum (the King's wife) .... _____

Birbal (advisor to the King) .... _____

Stranger .... _____

Merchant .... _____

Akhbar the King

Narrator	Birbal
Akhbar	Stranger
Begum	Merchant

Narrator: A long, long time ago, in a kingdom far away, there was a king by the name of Akhbar. He was a kindhearted king who cared deeply about his subjects. Nevertheless, Akhbar had some very unusual ideas about how to rule his kingdom, and this caused the royal court some concern.

Begum: Birbal, I've been very worried about Akhbar of late.

Birbal: Yes, he has a most peculiar habit of wandering about the streets dressed like a common beggar. This is not fitting for a king.

Begum: Do you think he is all right in the head?

Birbal: That's a good question. Oh, here he comes now. Let's approach the subject cautiously. Lions and madmen alike are unpredictable.

Akhbar: *(entering)* Good evening, my dear wife. Blessings on you too, Birbal.

Begum: What a fine coincidence. We were just talking about you!

Akhbar: Is that so? Pray tell the matter.

Birbal: To be frank, your behavior lately has been, how shall we say . . . less than royal.

Akhbar: Oh, so you've finally seen me out on the streets? Don't worry, my dear ones. I like to walk about in disguise. That way, I can see how the people really live, and hear what they say.

Begum: Is that why you've been acting like a lunatic? I don't know whether I should be relieved or even more alarmed.

Birbal: We certainly commend your interest in the people, but there are better ways to collect this information. Why don't we send out some spies?

Akhbar: I would rather see with my own eyes and hear with my own ears.

Birbal: Your Majesty, it is decidedly unsafe for you to be walking around town without protection. The streets are filled with urchins and hooligans.

Akhbar: I'll consider what you've said. After all, I know you care for me as much as I care for you.

Narrator: Birbal and Begum were somewhat appeased, but Akhbar continued his strange behavior. Then, one day, King Akhbar noticed somebody following him through the market. At first he was disturbed, then he became indignant. He suddenly turned to face the stranger.

Akhbar: Why are you following me?

Stranger: *(in a croaky voice)* Why not? The streets are free.

Akhbar: What's your name?

Stranger: Call me what you will.

Akhbar: Where do you live?

Stranger: Wherever I pitch my tent.

Akhbar: This is preposterous! Do you have any idea who you are talking to?

Stranger: A fool, apparently.

Akhbar: You are sadly mistaken. I am none other than Akhbar the King. If you don't believe me, gaze upon the royal seal that I wear here on my finger.

Narrator: The stranger peered for a moment at the seal, and then he grabbed it. In the blink of an eye, he was running through the market with the King's seal. Akhbar hollered for help. A merchant up the way heard the commotion.

Akhbar: *(faintly, in the distance)* Thief! Thief! Stop that man!

Merchant: What's that? Someone shouting in the streets, and another running this way? I'd better stop him and find out what's going on.

Narrator: The merchant stuck his foot out and tripped the stranger, who rolled over onto his side.

Stranger: How dare you! I am none other than Akhbar the King. If you don't believe me, look at the royal seal on my finger.

Merchant: Forgive me, Your Highness!

Stranger: Quit your mumbling and go get that madman shouting his head off. He's out of his mind!

Merchant: Yes, Your Highness. *(shouting to the crowd)* Come on, everybody! Help me get that beggar—he's insulted the King!

Narrator: Akhbar saw the crowd surging forward and ran for his life. He ran this way and that, ditching the mob. From a window high in the palace, Begum and Birbal watched him running through a secret passageway near the palace gates.

Akhbar: *(panting)* I made it!

Begum: Welcome home, dear. You're just in time for dinner.

Akhbar: I've never been so glad to hear those words.

Begum: Why don't you let Birbal help you out of those rags?

Akhbar: Birbal, you were so right about my wanderings with the common people. I truly could be harmed! Forgive me for not heeding your advice.

Birbal: You are quite forgiven. Thank the heavens you have returned home safely. Here is your royal robe, along with your seal.

Akhbar: Thank you, Bir—my royal seal! How did you get it? A thief snatched it from me just a few moments ago.

Birbal: Don't you know, Majesty, that I'm a master of disguise myself.

Akhbar: Birbal! It was you!

Birbal: I hope you learned your lesson.

Begum: A king's place is in his palace, not the market.

Akhbar: *(chuckling)* You have both taught me a very good lesson, indeed.

A Map of the Kingdom

In the space provided, draw a map of Akhbar's kingdom. Be sure to show Akhbar's palace, the palace gates, and the market. Draw arrows to show the route Akhbar took through the market and back home.

Story Map

What are the main elements of "Akhbar the King"? Complete the story map to summarize the play.

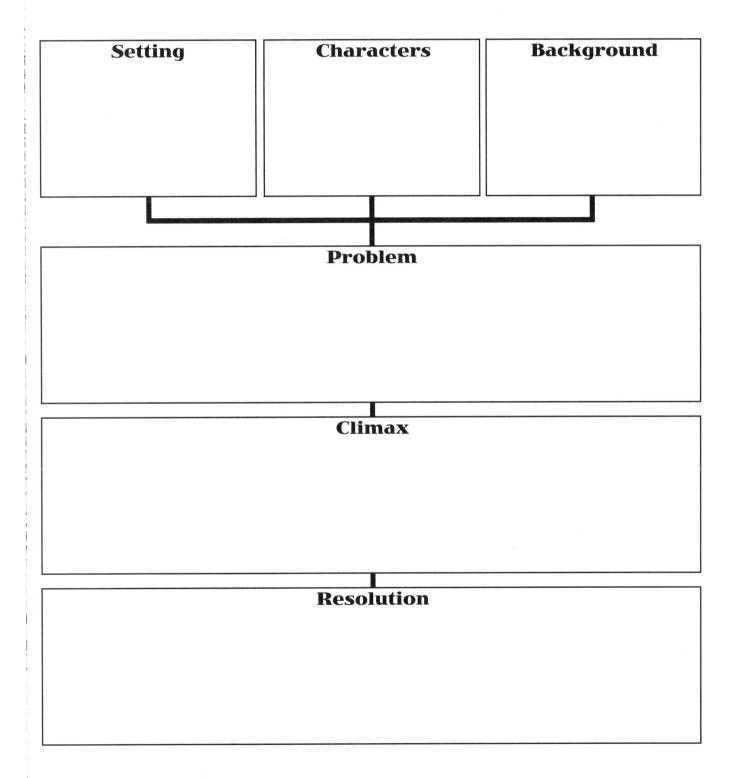

Setting	Characters	Background

Problem

Climax

Resolution

Opposites Attract

The following table shows words taken from the play. For each word, write a word in the second column that means the same or almost the same. In the third column, write a word that means the opposite.

Word	Synonym	Antonym
cautiously		
commend		
indignant		
peculiar		
preposterous		
relieved		
unpredictable		

Now write sentences using seven different words from the chart.

1. _____

2. _____

3. _____

4. _____

5. _____

6. _____

7. _____

Now Presenting...

Flowers from Topaz

In the aftermath of Pearl Harbor, the Fujishima family is transported to a relocation center for Japanese Americans. At the infamous camp known as Topaz, Reiko and her mother decide to start a class in the traditional Japanese art of ikebana, or flower arrangement.

7 parts

Setting the Stage

Background

Tell students that this script presents a fictional story based on real events. In 1941 the United States declared war on Japan after the Japanese attack on Pearl Harbor. The U.S. government arrested and detained Japanese Americans in California for suspicion of colluding—or cooperating—with Japan. There was never any evidence to support these charges of treason, and yet many Japanese Americans were detained for several years. One priority of the detainees was to continue their education and cultural traditions in the face of imprisonment. This play presents a fictional example of one family's attempt to uplift themselves in these dire circumstances.

Staging

The following items may be used as props at appropriate moments in the play: a vase with flowers, a radio, a suitcase, and badges or whistles for the agent and guard.

Encore

After reading this play, students may be inspired to try their hand at flower arrangement. It is not necessary to purchase flowers for this activity—have students collect materials on a walk: fallen branches, sprigs, pebbles, and other natural objects are all suitable for using in *ikebana*. Encourage students to think of this as an experiment in sculpture, which is in keeping with the art of ikebana.

Vocabulary

Be sure students are familiar with the meanings of the following words. Have partners create mini-dialogs using these words and then present them to the class.

arrest: to take into custody by authority of the law

assembly: a group of persons gathered together

barracks: a building or group of buildings, usually for housing soldiers

identification: anything used to establish a person's identity

improvisation: something created with the materials at hand, without special forethought

monotonous: tiresome; having little variation

relocation: the act of moving to a new location

traitor: a person who betrays his or her nation

transport: to carry over a long distance, from one place to another

Now Presenting...

Flowers from Topaz

When the U.S. declares war on Japan, Reiko and her parents are sent to a relocation camp for Japanese Americans. As time goes by, they start to think of ways they can spend their time usefully.

Characters

Narrator .... _____

Reiko Fujishima .... _____
(a 13-year-old girl)

Saburo Fujishima .... _____
(Reiko's father)

Michi Fujishima .... _____
(Reiko's mother)

Radio Announcer .... _____

Government Agent .... _____

Prison Guard .... _____

Flowers from Topaz

······················· **Characters** ·······················

Narrator   Radio Announcer
Reiko Fujishima   Government Agent
Saburo Fujishima   Prison Guard
Michi Fujishima

···

Narrator: In Japan the art of arranging flowers is known as *ikebana*. Reiko's grandmother was a master of ikebana, and she taught Reiko's mother everything she knew. When Reiko's parents moved to Oakland, California, her mother started giving ikebana lessons at home. As our play opens, Reiko is working on a flower arrangement with her mother at the kitchen table. While they work, they listen to the radio. The date is December 7, 1941. The musical program is interrupted by an emergency broadcast.

Radio Announcer: We interrupt this program with a news alert. Japanese warplanes attacked the U.S. Naval Base at Pearl Harbor early this morning . . .

Michi: Saburo! Come in here, quickly!

Saburo: *(entering)* What's the matter?

Michi: Shhh! Listen.

Radio Announcer: The Japanese air raid on Pearl Harbor came as a complete surprise. U.S. sailors and airmen were caught off guard, and a large part of the U.S. Naval Fleet has been lost . . .

Reiko: Oh no. I hope Uncle Takahashi is all right. He was stationed at Pearl Harbor.

Radio Announcer: President Roosevelt's reaction was swift. He immediately declared war on Japan. The United States will now be fighting the war on two fronts—in Europe as well as the Pacific . . .

Michi: Reiko, turn down the radio for now. Saburo, what do you think we should do?

Saburo: We should get ready to help in any way we can. There will probably be food drives, and the Red Cross will be asking for blood. We just need to do whatever is asked.

Reiko: Will everything be all right?

Saburo: Don't worry, Reiko. Whatever happens, we will face it together.

Narrator: Several months later, there was a loud knock on the Fujishima's front door. They could tell it wasn't going to be good news.

Michi: *(opening door)* Yes?

Agent: Are you Mrs. Fujishima?

Michi: Yes, I am. How can I help you?

Agent: May I please talk to your husband?

Saburo: Here I am. What seems to be the problem?

Agent: I'm here to inform you that you and your family are under arrest. The United States is at war with Japan, and all Japanese are under suspicion.

Saburo: That doesn't make any sense. The United States is at war with Germany and Italy too. Are you going to arrest all the Germans and Italians in the United States?

Agent: I'm the one asking questions here, not you. Now pack your bags and get ready to go. We're taking you to an assembly center. Other Japanese are being detained there too. Now hurry up!

Reiko: *(whispering)* Mom, what should I take with me?

Michi: Fill your suitcase with as much as you can, and wear a jacket over your sweater. There's no telling how long we'll be gone.

Narrator: The Fujishimas were transported to a bus station in downtown Oakland, where dozens of other Japanese American families were waiting. They all boarded a bus, which took them to a relocation center in Utah. The name of the camp was Topaz. When they arrived, Reiko was shocked.

Reiko: This is terrible. It looks like a prison camp. There are rows and rows of barracks. I can't see anything for hundreds of miles except dirt. What kind of a place is this?

Michi: Be quiet, Reiko. A guard is waving to us.

Guard: Step this way. What's your name?

Saburo: Fujishima.

Guard: Your identification number is 014921. Don't forget it.

Saburo: We won't.

Guard: Go to the unit at the end of Opal Avenue. That's where you'll be staying. *(leaves)*

Reiko: How can they call this an avenue? It's just a dirt path.

Saburo: Reiko, don't let them hear you complain. We'll have to make the best of it.

Narrator: Although they had broken no laws, the Japanese Americans at Topaz were treated like traitors. They lived in barracks that were furnished with nothing but cots and a table. They had no running water or electricity. The camp officials enforced many rules, but provided no education or activities for the children. The days stretched into weeks, and the weeks became months. Life in the camp was dull and monotonous.

Michi: Reiko, I think it's time we find something for you to do. We may be here for a while.

Reiko: I've been thinking the same thing. You know what I miss the most? The times we used to spend doing ikebana.

Michi: Those are good memories, aren't they? Listen, why don't we practice ikebana here?

Reiko: How? There isn't a flower for miles around.

Michi: You shouldn't give up so easily, Reiko. A true artist uses whatever materials are available. Let's take this box and see what we can find.

Narrator: Reiko and her mother went on a walk, filling the box with things they found along the way. Suddenly, they were stopped by a guard.

Guard: Halt! Give me your identification.

Michi: Fujishima. 014921.

Guard: What are you doing?

Michi: We're just cleaning up the camp. See? There's nothing in here except garbage.

Guard: Hmmm . . . Well, all right. Be on your way.

Narrator: Later that afternoon, Reiko and her mother sorted through the things they had collected.

Michi: Look, Reiko. These dry old branches can be used as stems. We could fold these scraps of paper in the shape of flowers and twist them around the branches.

Reiko: We collected a lot of nice pebbles too. I'll arrange them in this tray. That will form the base.

Michi: Good idea. Here, let me help you.

Reiko: I never thought I would have to come to a place like Topaz to learn such an important lesson about ikebana. Now I can see that it's true: you can use almost anything to make a thing of beauty.

Michi: Improvisation is the heart and soul of ikebana. You just need to use your imagination.

Narrator: Soon after that, Reiko and her mother started an ikebana class at Topaz. They taught the art of flower arrangement every Thursday afternoon for the next three years. Finally, in December 1944, President Roosevelt announced the closing of relocation camps. Thousands of Japanese Americans returned to California, only to find that they had lost their homes. Of all those who were imprisoned in the relocation camps, there was not a single case of a Japanese American being disloyal to the United States.

Name _____

A Flower Arrangement

Now is your chance to try your own hand at *ikebana*. In the vase provided, draw an arrangement of flowers. You may want to include a variety of other natural objects such as branches, leaves, or dry flowers. Label each of the items in your drawing.

Name _____

Teaching Plan

What kind of class would you want to start at Topaz? Complete the following form to help you organize your teaching plan.

1. Name of Class:

   _____

   _____

2. Name of Instructor:

   _____

   _____

3. Required Materials:

   _____

   _____

4. Important Topics or Concepts:

   _____

   _____

   _____

   _____

5. Sample Lesson Plan:

   _____

   _____

   _____

   _____

Now Presenting...

The Great Transcontinental Railroad Race

Two railroad companies are in a historic race to see which one can lay the most track in the least amount of time. In the end, teamwork will distinguish the winner from the loser.

Setting the Stage

Background

Tell students that this play is about the building of the Transcontinental Railroad. Before 1870 there were no railroads west of the Mississippi. Cross-country travel could take weeks or even months. President Lincoln personally promoted the idea of rail construction throughout the western regions, calling it a political necessity. The Pacific Railroad Act was passed in 1862, specifying the Central Pacific Railroad Company and the Union Pacific Railroad Company as contractors. The Act specified that the two companies construct a line connecting Sacramento and Omaha. However, it gave no guidelines on how the work was to be divided. Both companies were spurred to build as much as they could, as quickly as possible, thereby gaining all the glory—and hopefully making lots of money in the process.

Staging

Give students spoons or other metal implements. They may tap them together at appropriate moments in the play to mimic the sound of hammers and spikes.

Encore

After reading this script, students may enjoy learning more about the legendary John Henry. They may read some of the known facts about him, as well as learn about the legend and check out lyrics for the folk ballad on the John Henry Internet site (www.ibiblio.org/john_henry/henry.html).

Vocabulary

Be sure students are familiar with the meanings of the following words. To check comprehension, give students a synonym or a definition for each term and then have them identify the correct vocabulary word.

achieve: to accomplish or succeed in doing something

ambitious: demanding great effort and skill

exhausting: extremely tiring

feat: accomplishment

interval: a space between two things

province: a part of the country distant from the capital

Now Presenting...

The Great Transcontinental Railroad Race

Two railroad companies: one working west, and one working east. Which one can lay the most track in the least amount of time?

Characters

Narrator................................... _____

James Strobridge...................... _____
(construction boss)

Charles Crocker (overseer)....... _____

Michael Shay (laborer)............. _____

Fusang Li (laborer)................... _____

Cato Haywood (laborer)........... _____

Photographer .... _____

The Great Transcontinental Railroad Race

.... **Characters** ....

Narrator

James Strobridge

Charles Crocker

Michael Shay

Fusang Li

Cato Haywood

Photographer

Narrator: In 1863 two railroad companies began the most ambitious railway project to date. The Central Pacific Railroad Company started laying track east of Sacramento. In Omaha, the Union Pacific Railroad Company started laying track in a western direction. The two tracks were to meet somewhere between California and Nebraska. The company that worked fastest would get the most work, and therefore the most money. The race was on to finish the Transcontinental Railroad.

Strobridge: *(entering)* Afternoon, Crocker. I've got news from the tracks, if you can take it.

Crocker: *(motioning to a chair)* That doesn't sound good. Tell it to me, whatever it is.

Strobridge: Well, the Union Pacific is gaining ground. It set a new record of seven miles, eighteen hundred feet today.

Crocker: Blasted! In that case, we'll set a record of our own. Stro', I want you and the men to lay ten miles of track in one day.

Strobridge: Ten miles! In one day? It can't be done.

Crocker: Never say never, my dear fellow.

 Readers' Theater, Grade 6 • EMC 3311

Strobridge: Miracles don't come cheap. At the rate you're talking, we'll need a lot more men. And another thing—they'll want more money to work like packhorses all day long.

Crocker: Tell them we'll pay four times their normal wages, as long as they break the record.

Narrator: The big day finally arrived. To meet the challenge, Central Pacific hired thousands of men. These workers represented the best laborers that Central Pacific could find. At 7 a.m. on April 28, 1869, a shrill whistle announced the start of the work day. This particular day would be anything but ordinary, however. It was a day that would go down in history.

Strobridge: Harness the horses, crew. They'll pull the flat cars to the end of the track.

Shay: Got it, boss. Here, Fusang. Take these spikes and put them on top of the rails on the flat car.

Fusang: Uuff! Those are heavy. All right, everything's loaded.

Strobridge: Remember, to lay ten miles of track in one day, you'll have to lay more than one mile of track per hour. Now get going!

Narrator: As the flat car moved forward, rails and spikes were spilled onto the ground. Meanwhile, workers prepared a bed of gravel. Wooden ties were placed across the gravel at regular intervals. The rails were laid over the ties and joined with iron plates, one rail in front of the other. Workers pounded spikes into the ties to secure the rails in place. When the rails and spikes were all used up, the flat cars went back for more. It was exhausting work. To keep their spirits up, the workers told jokes and sang songs. They all took different parts in these songs.

(The following lines are chanted in a singsong call-and-response rhythm.)

Strobridge: John Henry was a railroad man; he worked from six 'til five.

Haywood: "Raise up the rails and let 'em drop down; I'll beat any man alive."

Strobridge: John Henry said to his captain—

Haywood: "You are nothing but a lazy man; before that steam drill shall beat me down, I'll die with my hammer in my hand."

Strobridge: John Henry's captain said to him—

Shay: "I believe these mountains are caving in."

Strobridge: John Henry said to his captain—

Haywood: "Oh, Lord! That's my hammer you hear in the wind."

Strobridge: John Henry he said to his captain—

Haywood: "Your money is getting mighty tight. When I hammer in the very last spike, will you pay me what you owe tonight?"

Strobridge: John Henry's captain came to him with fifty dollars in his hand. He laid his hand on his shoulder and said—

Shay: "This belongs to a steel-driving man."

Strobridge: John Henry was hammering on the right side; the big steam drill on the left. Before that steam drill could beat him down, he hammered himself to death. John Henry was lying on his death bed; he turned over on his side. And these were the last words John Henry said—

Haywood: *(slowly, in a very deep voice)* "Bring me a cool drink of water before I die."

(End song.)

Crocker: That was a good one. Speaking of cold water, let's take a break.

Narrator: While they ate lunch, a photographer walked among them, taking pictures and asking questions.

Photographer: Sit closer together. That's it. Now don't move. *(flashbulb flashes)* Thank you, all.

Haywood: Are we going to be in the papers tomorrow?

Photographer: Could be. The whole country's waiting to see if you can really do this.

Haywood: Well, save yourself some time and print the story. It's as good as done.

Photographer: Where are you from?

Haywood: I was a slave down in South Carolina. But when the Civil War ended a few years back, I came up north looking for work. That's when I heard about the Transcontinental Railroad. This here is my friend, Michael Shay.

Shay: That's right. Me and Cato worked together on the same plantation. I was a house servant, and mighty glad to get out of there when it was over.

Photographer: *(to Fusang)* And how about you? Where are you from?

Fusang: I'm from Kwantung. It's a province in China on the Canton Delta.

Photographer: You can speak English pretty well for a Chinaman.

Fusang: That's why Mr. Strobridge chose me as the headman for my gang. There's a lot of Chinese working here. The railroad needs interpreters like me to tell them what to do!

Strobridge: All right men, quit your lollygaggin' and head on out! It's after 2 in the afternoon. We've only got four or five hours of sunlight left.

Narrator: Up ahead was the crew's biggest challenge. They had to lay tracks up and over the Promontory Mountains. The slope was steep and full of curves, so the rails had to be bent. The men had to walk over the steep hillside themselves, because the horses had collapsed from exhaustion. The workers kept pounding spikes, with a determination that couldn't be shaken. At sunset, Strobridge signaled for the final blast from the train whistle. They had done it!

Crocker: Strobridge, I can't believe you did it! The final measurements are in—your men put down ten miles, fifty-seven feet of rail today. John Henry himself would be impressed.

Strobridge: You're darn tootin'. Crew, give yourselves a holler.

Shay, Li, and Haywood: Yeee-haw!

Narrator: On May 10, 1869, the Central Pacific and Union Pacific Railroad Companies joined tracks. The country was now linked by a transcontinental railroad, and the West would never be the same. Central Pacific's crew had proven that momentous feats of labor *could* be achieved with some good old-fashioned teamwork.

Name _____

10-Mile Math

Study the measurements below. Then answer the questions.

```
12 inches = 1 foot
3 feet = 1 yard
1,760 yards = 1 mile
```

1. Central Pacific laid 10 miles, fifty-seven feet of track. How many feet is that in all?

   _____

2. How can you express that same measurement in yards?

   _____

3. The crew used a total of 3,520 rails. If an iron plate is fastened to both ends of each rail, how many plates did they use?

   _____

4. A set of two nuts and bolts are used for each iron plate. How many nuts and bolts were used in total?

   _____

5. Four spikes are used for each rail. How many spikes is that in all?

   _____

6. The crew started at 7:30 a.m. and ended at 7 p.m. If they took a lunch break that lasted one and a half hours, how many hours did they work in all?

   _____

7. In that case, how many yards of track did they lay per hour?

   _____

Name _____

Map of the West

This map shows the Transcontinental Railroad and state borders as they are today. How well do you know this region? Write the name of each state in its place.

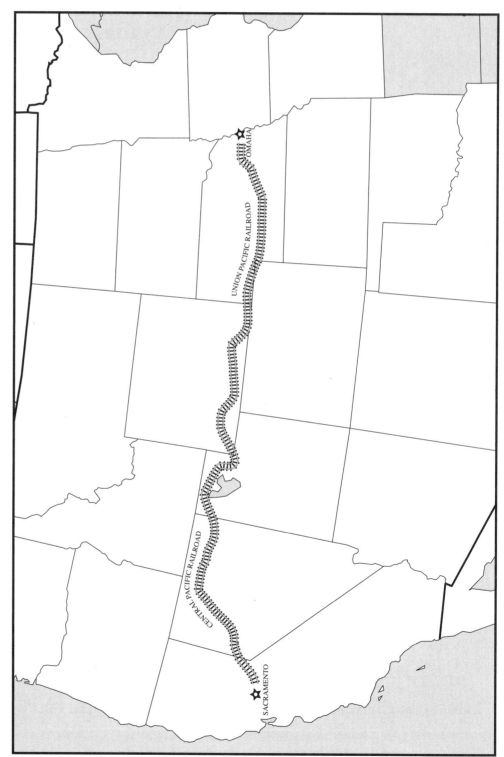

Arizona	California	Idaho
Iowa	Kansas	Missouri
Montana	Nebraska	New Mexico
North Dakota	Oklahoma	South Dakota
Texas	Utah	Wyoming
	Colorado	
	Minnesota	
	Nevada	
	Oregon	
	Washington	

Answer Key

Golem

page 14: 1. The setting is Prague, the capital of Czechoslovakia. The year is 1592.; 2. Christians are falsely accusing Jews of horrible crimes. The Jews fear for their lives.; 3. He decides to hold a fake trial. He wants to punish Isaac, a Jewish baker, because he thinks or hopes that the enemies of the Jews will be satisfied with this.; 4. He has secret knowledge that allows him to create human life out of raw material.; 5. He didn't know what the charges against him were. Plus, there was no evidence presented at the trial.; 6. Possible answers: Yes. There was no other way to get the Emperor to change his mind; No. The Rabbi did not approve of violence. He probably just wanted Golem to rescue Isaac without hurting anybody.; 7. Possible answer: Golem was aware of the difference between life and death. When he asks, "What will happen to Golem?" you can tell that he is worried about his own life.

page 15: **The Moral of the Story:** Revenge is not a solution to violence. It only leads to destruction. **Reason:** Possible answers—Golem was only supposed to rescue the Jews, not get revenge. Rabbi Leib warned everyone not to resort to violence. **Personal Reaction:** Answers will vary. Some students may agree that violence only leads to more violence and therefore should be avoided at all costs. Others may feel that some situations do indeed call for violence. Remind students to support their answers with reasons and examples.

page 16: Sample Answers: Emperor=President of the United States; Rabbi Leib=Top Scientist of the U.S.; Golem=Automated Cop I. African Americans are falsely accused by New York City police of crimes they did not commit.; II. The president asks for help from a leading scientist.; III. The scientist creates a whole police force of automated cops who are incapable of "racial profiling."; IV. The robots arrest people in record numbers for every conceivable violation.; V. The president tells the scientist he has to program some "common sense" into the robots.; VI. The scientist responds that only human beings are capable of common sense. Human cops return to the job with greater sensitivity.

Welcome to Ellis Island

page 24: Sample paragraph: After entering the main building, immigrants to Ellis Island had to check in their bags. Then they went up a stairway to the Great Hall. They had to undergo both a medical exam and a legal inspection. If they passed these examinations without any problems, they were allowed to change their money into U.S. dollars and leave the building.

page 25: 1. Germany 7,142,393; 2. Mexico 5,542,625; 3. Italy 5,427,298; 4. United Kingdom 5,225,701; 5. Ireland 4,778,159; 6. Canada 4,423,066; 7. Soviet Union (former) 3,752,811; 8. Austria 1,841,068; 9. Hungary 1,673,579; Philippines 1,379,403; Total for All Countries 41,186,103
1. 29,841,009; 2. 9,965,691; 3. 234,011.95

Whiz Kid

page 32: 1. batch of cookies; 2. cast of characters; 3. colony of ants; 4. cord of wood; 5. herd of cattle; 6. kettle of hawks; 7. pod of whales; 8. pride of lions; 9. ream of paper; 10. swarm of bees

page 33: 1. 210 minutes; 2. Mt. Everest; 3. collective nouns; 4. a closed geometric figure with straight sides; 5. quadrilaterals; 6. a geometric figure with six sides; 7. 29 bones; 8. 100 zeroes

page 34: Check students' work for accuracy. Have students provide their sources. Help them rewrite their questions and answers if they are not clearly phrased or if they are inaccurate. After partners have finished role-playing an episode of "Whiz Quiz," you may also wish to play the game as a group. Form teams and collect students' work. Read from students' activity sheets to quiz each team, and keep score on the board.

Romeo and Juliet

page 42: Answers will vary. Students may write a message to the lovers in the form of a brief statement, or it may take the form of a poem. The message may tell of the peace Romeo and Juliet brought to the two families, or it may praise the purity of their love.

page 43: Answers will vary. Sample answer: Love is a very turbulent emotion. In fact, it's not just one emotion but a bunch of emotions all rolled into one. It is passion, sorrow, and insanity all at once. It can be very sweet and tender, but it can also leave a bitter taste in your mouth.

A Trip to Mars

page 51: Sample answer: The United States sent its first space probe to Mars in 1965. *Mariner 4* took photos of Mars' surface. It was followed by *Mariner 6, Mariner 7,* and *Mariner 9.* In total, the *Mariner* missions took more than 7,000 photos of Mars. The *Viking* missions were the first to land on Mars. They analyzed rock samples and climate. *Pathfinder* collected further samples, expanding our knowledge of the planet. The *Mars Global Surveyor* was launched in 1996, at about the same time as *Pathfinder.* Its goal was to photograph and map all of Mars.

page 52: Example: A recent mission to Mars has revealed that life once existed there. Evidence suggests this life was no more complex than simple microbes. A global climate change froze all forms of life on Mars millions of years ago. These discoveries were made by Captain Powell and shipmates Walker and Jackson. They mixed Martian soil with water and discovered that the frozen microbes came to life.

Kids, Unite!

page 59: 1a. 13 x $0.01 = $0.13; b. $0.13 x 5 = $0.65; c. $0.65 x 4 = $2.60; 2a. $5.15 x 3 = $15.45; b. $15.45 x 4 = $61.80; c. $61.80 x 4 = $247.20; 3a. ($17.00 x 7.5) x 5 = $637.50; b. $637.50 x 4 = $2,550; c. $2,550 x 12 = $30,600

page 60: 1. factory; 2. union; 3. management; 4. grievance; 5. boss; 6. strike; 7. picket; 8. negotiate

page 61: Answers will vary. Share with students the following ideas, which have been taken and adapted from the Universal Declaration of Human Rights: 1. Everyone has the right to work.; 2. Nobody should be forced to work.; 3. No one shall be held in slavery.; 4. Workers have the right to safe working conditions.; 5. All people have the right to equal pay for equal work.; 6. Workers have the right to a minimum wage.; 7. Workers have the right to form and join unions.

Balancing Act

page 68: 1. An overly simple picture of a person. A collection of traits or characteristics used to describe a "type" of person.; 2. Judging a person based on his or her appearance or background.; 3. Hatred of gays and lesbians.; 4. Points of view that limit men and women to certain roles.; 5. Prejudice and discrimination against people of a different color or race.; 6. The peaceful coexistence of people of different colors, religions, backgrounds, and lifestyles.

page 69: Possible answers include constructive comments, such as: **Lee:** Why don't you try it? It takes a lot of courage to do gymnastics. **Jerome:** I'm going to hang out with Lee. I don't care what you think. **Amber:** Actually, I won the election because I worked really hard for it.

page 70: Answers will vary. Possibilities include: 1. It doesn't feel good to be called names. You should think how it feels before you put somebody down because of the way he or she looks.; 2. Stereotypes are usually negative. Thinking in terms of stereotypes makes you a negative person.; 3. People are much more complicated than a simple stereotype. Prejudice is just too simplistic, even for children.; 4. Stereotypes are often based on fear and hatred. They give distorted pictures of people that aren't true.; 5. Prejudice can easily escalate into violence, even war.

Sarah Winnemucca: A Leader for Peace

page 78: 1. The setting is Camp McDermit in Nevada. The year is 1866.; 2. Sarah and her brother learn that a Paiute has been killed by a soldier for possessing gunpowder.; 3. The army would punish them and maybe even take more lives.; 4. He is greedy and cowardly. He sells the Paiutes things that he is supposed to give them for free, and he runs away at the slightest sign of danger.; 5. He tells Sarah that he will give the Paiutes the provisions they need if she and Natchez bring their father back to the reservation.; 6. She is bilingual, so she can communicate with both the whites and the Paiutes.; She is good at negotiating, and seeks the opinions of others before offering her own suggestions.; 7. Possible answers: Native Americans were forced onto the reservations—they were not presented with any other options.; The reservations are often located in poor, undeveloped, and unproductive lands.

page 79: 8, 1, 5, 7, 4, 6, 9, 2, 3

Arachne's Web

page 86: Students may choose a variety of scenes to illustrate, but their drawings should depict either the myth of Echo and Hera, or the myth of Echo and Narcissus.

page 87: 1. Athena is angry at Arachne for not paying her respect and for bragging about herself. In particular, she's mad that Arachne said she is an even better weaver than Athena.; 2. No, Arachne would not be afraid to give a speech in public. She is very self-confident and has no problem displaying her talents in front of others.; 3. Athena tells the story of Hera and Echo, who was punished for talking too much. Arachne then tells how Echo fell in love with Narcissus, who was in turn punished for his vanity.; 4. *Narcissistic* means "to be excessively vain or in love with oneself.".; 5. Possible answer: The ancient Greeks placed a great deal of importance on respect for authority.; 6. Answers will vary.; 7. Possible answer: The Greeks invented their myths to explain the world around them. The myths provided solutions to the mysteries of nature.

page 88: Possible answers—**Athena:** powerful, authoritarian, vengeful; **Arachne:** proud, defiant, talented; **Echo:** talkative, naive, impulsive; **Narcissus:** handsome, vain, egotistical

Muhammad Ali v. the U.S. Draft

page 96: 1964 Cassius Clay wins world heavyweight title in a fight with Sonny Liston. He converts to Islam and changes his name to Muhammad Ali.
1967 Ali refuses to be inducted into the U.S. Army. He is convicted of draft evasion and banned from boxing.
1970 Court order overturns Ali's suspension from boxing. He returns to the ring in a fight with Jerry Quarry.
1971 The Supreme Court reverses Ali's conviction for resisting the draft.
1981 Ali retires from boxing.
1984 Ali is diagnosed with Parkinson's disease.

page 97: Sample slogans for Doves: Fight Racism, not the Vietnamese; U.S. Out of Vietnam; War Is Not the Answer; Wage Peace
Sample slogans for Hawks: Stop Communism!; Proud to Be American; It's U.S. Against THEM; The U.S.—Love It or Leave It

To Tell the Truth

page 105: Possible answers: 2. She actually lives in Livermore, California.; 3. Actually, she's a clerk at the T-Mart.; 4. She really doesn't have a boyfriend at all.; 5. She's really average-looking.; 6. Her mother is actually a waitress.; 7. In fact, she is very insecure.; 8. She actually cares a lot about other people's opinions—too much, in fact.

page 106: Part I: 1. gorgeous; 2. beautiful; 3. pretty; 4. plain; 5. unattractive; 6. ugly; 7. hideous; Part II: 1. undeniable; 2. true; 3. probable; 4. questionable; 5. unlikely; 6. false; 7. deceptive

The *Amistad* Case

page 114: 1. Cause: Fifty-three Africans are kidnapped by slave traders.
    Effect: They kill the crew on board.
2. Cause: A U.S. Navy ship discovers the *Amistad* off the coast of New York.
    Effect: Cinqué and his fellow countrymen are taken to a courtroom in New York.
3. Cause: Attorney Baldwin presents overwhelming evidence in favor of the defendants.
    Effect: Cinqué and the others are found not guilty of murder and mutiny.
4. Cause: President Van Buren orders a retrial.
    Effect: The *Amistad* case is taken to the Supreme Court.
5. Cause: John Quincy Adams argues the case very effectively in court.
    Effect: Cinqué and the others are granted their freedom.
6. Cause: Cinqué raises money by giving lectures.
    Effect: The Africans can at last afford the return trip to Sierra Leone.

page 115:

	Trial Court	Supreme Court
Prosecutor's Argument	The defendants are guilty of mutiny and murder	The defendants are slaves and are the property of Spain. They should be returned to Spain and tried in a Spanish court.
Defense's Argument	The court does not have any authority to rule in this case.	The defendants were born free and have a right to their freedom.
Verdict	The defendants should be returned to their homeland at the expense of the U.S. government.	The defendants had a right to fight back and should be set free. The U.S. government is not obligated to pay for their return to Sierra Leone, however.